THE POSTWAR WORLD

THE POSTWAR WORLD

The Merrick Lectures for 1944
Ohio Wesleyan University

By
HASTINGS EELLS
ROBERT S. LYND
JOSEPH L. HROMÁDKA
T. A. BISSON
FRANCIS B. SAYRE
Y. C. YANG
VERA MICHELES DEAN
HENRY A. ATKINSON
JOHN L. CHILDS
H. GORDON HAYES
CLAIR WILCOX
MANLEY O. HUDSON
HAROLD H. BURTON

ABINGDON-COKESBURY PRESS
New York • Nashville

THE POSTWAR WORLD

COPYRIGHT, MCMXLV
By WHITMORE & STONE

Wartime Books

Wartime shortage of pulp, manpower, and transportation has produced a severe shortage of paper. In compliance with orders of the War Production Board, wartime books are printed on lighter-weight paper. This reduces thickness and weight. New books have more words to the page and smaller margins. This reduces the number of pages without reducing reading content.

Thinner books save paper, critical copper, and other metals. They help also to avoid wartime increases in book prices. Wartime books appear to be smaller, but their content has not been cut. They are complete. The only change is in appearance.

SET UP, PRINTED, AND BOUND BY THE PARTHENON PRESS AT NASHVILLE, TENNESSEE, UNITED STATES OF AMERICA

CONTENTS

THE POSTWAR WORLD

THE DIFFICULTIES OF MAKING PEACE

Hastings Eells

Professor of History, Ohio Wesleyan University

EVERY GOOD AMERICAN WANTS HIS COUNTRY TO WIN THIS WAR and never fight another one. We want a lasting peace, but how? The answer to that question is not easy. Nevertheless one thing is clear. This war came about because there was something terribly wrong with the prewar world. If another world conflict is to be avoided, it is vitally important to construct a different and better postwar world. It is not enough to beat down the enemy. We must build up the world, including the enemy. This will take planning.

Before we start planning it is well to remember that no surgeon performs an operation without making every effort to learn how that operation has been performed by other surgeons. No lawyer argues a case until he has studied carefully how that type of case has been argued in the past. No good general leads an army into battle until after he has retraced the movements of other armies in the great battles of history. Why, then, should any man feel qualified to offer advice on how peace shall be made at the end of this war until he has studied the history of the making of peace?

Unfortunately, the story of peacemaking is a sad and sorry tale. It is startling to discover that mankind has not yet learned how to go about the making of a lasting peace. The last great world treaty, the Treaty of Versailles, was a failure in the sense that it did not prevent another world war. The next peace before that, the Treaty of Paris, 1856, was shattered after fifteen years. The Treaty of Vienna, 1815, the most successful of its kind, can be said to have lasted only thirty-three years at the most. And in this list of broken treaties must be included those of Paris, 1763, Utrecht, 1713, and Westphalia, 1648.

Why does the making of peace show this tragic record? The answer is not hard to find. Every peace treaty has faced five fundamental difficulties that have proved to be insoluble problems. These difficulties are (1) choosing the men to make the peace, (2) organizing the peace congress, (3) ending the war, (4) rebuilding the world, and (5) preserving the peace. It is the purpose of this lecture to show what each of these problems involves. The Treaty of Versailles will be used as an example, in order that the reader may have a historical basis for understanding the discussion of postwar plans in the lectures that follow.

I. Choosing the Men to Make the Peace

No peace can be bigger than the men who make it. It is not enough for them to hold high positions, exercise great powers, and perform elaborate ceremonies. They must be truly big in vision, in leadership, and in character. They must be brave enough to speak unpleasant truths, and honest enough to stand by the right regardless of the cost. Sending a man to a peace congress works no magic transformation. He is still human and still sees through a glass darkly, even if he does see more than most men.

The Congress of Paris, 1919, had no lack of numbers. There were some five hundred newspaper reporters, many of them well informed on world affairs; but most of them had a hard time getting even scraps of news, while very few were ever consulted on the decisions made. There were crowds of envoys and experts, well equipped with medals and libraries. Yet few of them did more than attend some pompous ceremonies and wait around while the real work of the congress went on behind closed doors. The decisions were made by a minority of the men who went to Paris; and there was nobody to represent the two largest and strongest countries on the continent of Europe, Germany and Russia. Germany was in disgrace, and Russia was waging war with the Allies. Maybe these were good reasons for excluding them, but nevertheless no treaty could be expected to have their support in which they were not given a full share. Without the support of these two great powers no treaty could possibly be lasting. They never forgot this insult, and they never forgave it.

II. Organizing the Peace Congress

Before discussing the work of the Congress of Paris, it is only fair to observe that the congress was under serious handicaps similar to those which every such assembly may expect to face. The end of the war was unexpected. The Allied generals had plans made for at least another year. The fighting did not stop with the armistice on November 11, 1918, as many people suppose. The Germans laid down their arms; but war continued to be waged in Russia, in Rumania, in Hungary, in Turkey, and in Poland. The world was in a hurry for peace, with little consideration for the enormous problems involved. None of the men at Paris had ever participated in the making of a world peace; and in addition they worked in an atmosphere of greed, hostility, and bitter bargaining that was almost another war.

Each nation came to the congress with a list of gains it intended to make, and one of the commonest tricks for getting them was "bargaining power." This meant making a demand which the nation knew would not be granted. Then the nation would yield on condition that it was given some other gain. This gain was what it really expected to get in the first place. For example, England demanded that the United States should discard the Monroe Doctrine, knowing very well that the Americans would never consent. Then the British offered to yield on this issue provided the United

States in return would agree that Great Britain should have a larger navy than the Americans. This was what the British really wanted. The Americans refused to yield on either point.

The organization for the Congress of Paris proved to be unworkable in large part. The congress opened on January 18, 1919, with a full assembly of all the delegates. There were only a few more meetings of the full assembly, and it did little more than act as a rubber stamp for decisions already made.

Most of the work of the congress was done by commissions, each of which investigated some special subject and made recommendations. One of the most important was the commission on the League of Nations. The commissions worked long and hard, yet this was no guarantee of success. The commission on reparations, for instance, was able to achieve only a temporary solution that did more harm than good, while other commissions produced results of questionable validity.

The final decisions were made by a Council of Ten, consisting of two statesmen from each of the five leading countries —France, Great Britain, Italy, the United States, and Japan. It proved unworkable. The Japanese seldom attended unless a matter concerning themselves was up for discussion. The Italians took little interest in any matters not related to Italy. Finally, in February, Wilson went back to America for a month; and the sessions of the Ten came to an end. On his return it was decided to have a Council of Four—Wilson from the United States, Lloyd George from Great Britain, Clemenceau from France, and Orlando from Italy. This was more workable until, in April, the Italians withdrew in anger from Paris; and that left a Council of Three. These three made the final decisions at the close of the congress. In reality it was one man who settled matters; for in practice what usually happened was that one of the Three would make a proposal, one other would support him, and then the settlement rested on whether the third man would give in or hold out. Perhaps such a situation was unavoidable; perhaps it was the right way to decide matters; yet even so it is staggering to think that the destiny of the whole world rested to such a large extent upon one man's fortitude or stubbornness.

The one man who did most of the deciding in this way was Woodrow Wilson. Wilson was by nature a lone eagle. He came to Europe under the handicap of a severe defeat in the recent elections for Congress, while Clemenceau and Lloyd George had their countries united behind them. Europe received Wilson with an orgy of adulation. Streets were named after him; big banquets were held in his honor; and in Rome the crowd that welcomed him was so tumultuous that Wilson himself became excited and threw kisses from the balcony to the people below. It is not strange that he made the grievous error of thinking that the people, the "good people," of Europe were ready to back him to the limit, when in reality they were only backing him as long as he handed out favors.

Three policies formed the foundation of Wilson's thinking at the Congress of Paris: the self-determination of nations, the League of Nations, and a single peace. There were two tasks to be done by the congress, each of a different nature. One was to end the war—that is, to stop the fighting, demobilize the armies, dismantle the fortresses, and return the prisoners to their homes. This could be done quickly and fairly easily. The other was to rebuild the world—to reconstruct devastated areas, draw new boundaries, and establish barriers against the outbreak of another war. This was extremely difficult and might be even endless. Each task required a different kind of treaty suited to its peculiar problems. Yet Wilson demanded just one treaty, because he was determined to have Europe adopt his plan of a League of Nations. He knew that if it was not adopted quickly it never would be; so he resorted to the stratagem of having just one

11

treaty of peace including the League of Nations. Thus, in order to make the treaty, and end the war, Europe would have to adopt the League.

For purposes of clear discussion it will be better to consider these two problems separately and to look first at the way in which the Congress of Paris tried to rebuild the world.

III. REBUILDING THE WORLD

Since rebuilding the world was a complicated task, it is impossible in this brief space to discuss all aspects of it. For the purpose of realizing the problem, it may be sufficient to survey three features of the Versailles Treaty, namely, boundaries, the League of Nations, and the silences of Versailles.

The problem of boundaries is a triple threat to any peace congress. This is because a nation has at least three kinds of boundaries: political (or nationalistic), economic, and strategic. The political boundaries must be drawn so as to include all the people who feel that they belong to the government of that nation and not to include any others. The economic boundaries must take in all the territory necessary to the nation's economic prosperity and security. For example, they must include sufficient agricultural country to provide plenty of food; enough mines to provide minerals, such as coal; and outlets to the sea for international trade. The strategic boundaries must take in all the points essential to preserving the security of the country, so that it shall be safe from attack and in a position to deal vigorously with any enemies. For example, the strategic boundaries of the United States include the Panama Canal. The economic boundaries extend to the rubber plantations of Malaya on the other side of the globe. And all that most maps show is the political boundaries.

To make these three kinds of boundaries coincide is impossible. To draw them correctly for one nation without injury to the demands of others is a hopeless task.

There were three sore spots treated by the "doctors" of

Versailles that illustrate the complexities of the boundary difficulty. One was the Polish Corridor. The Polish Corridor was the strip of territory along the Vistula River to the shore of the Baltic Sea which formed a broad avenue between Germany on the west and East Prussia on the other side. The population of the Corridor was thoroughly Polish except for its one and only good harbor, Danzig. This city was definitely German; and East Prussia was more German than Germany itself, even if it was separated from Germany by the Corridor. The problem was to re-establish the nation of Poland without forcing the Germans in Danzig and East Prussia to submit to the Poles. In other words, the political boundaries of Germany took in Danzig and East Prussia. The political boundary of Poland included the Corridor that lay between. Economically and strategically both countries wanted the Corridor.

The Congress of Paris made a patchwork settlement of the problem which pleased nobody and antagonized everybody. The Polish Corridor was given to Poland, partly because it was Polish and partly because it was Poland's only outlet to the sea. East Prussia was given to Germany. And Danzig was made a "free city." But Danzig didn't want to be a free city; it wanted to be part of Germany. Germany didn't like to be separated from East Prussia by the Corridor. And Poland was unhappy because the outlet to the sea was of little value without Danzig. It is small wonder, then, that the second World War officially began with a German invasion of the Polish Corridor on September 1, 1939.

Another sore spot was the Saar. The Saar was a small region on the border between France and Germany about half way between the North Sea and the Alps. Politically it belonged to Germany because it was inhabited by Germans. But economically it was desired by both countries. France wanted it because it had valuable coal mines, and France needed coal mines badly to replace those ruined by the Germans in the war. Strategically it was essential to the security of both countries because it was a mountainous area that could be very useful for defense. Clemenceau demanded that the Saar be given to France. Lloyd George was willing, although usually he opposed giving to one nation a district inhabited by a different nationality, since that might prove a cause for another war. Wilson positively refused to let France have the Saar. The result was a deadlock that dragged on for week after week.

Finally matters reached a climax on Saturday, March 28, at a meeting of the commission. Clemenceau remarked that the Saar had been part of France in 1814. Wilson retorted that that was a hundred years ago and a hundred years was a long time. Clemenceau quickly replied that a hundred years was indeed a long time—in a young nation like the United States. He suggested that Wilson might be called pro-German and indicated that France would not sign any treaty that did not give her the Saar. Wilson's temper was aroused. He had not missed the insinuation that the United States was a child among nations. He asked whether Clemenceau meant to say that if he didn't get what he wanted he would like to have the Americans go home. To which the French premier replied that he didn't want *them* to go home, but that *he* was going home right then, and stalked out of the room. The situation was critical. Wilson reported to the American delegation that afternoon that the congress might break up. A week later he adopted a suggestion by his close adviser, Colonel House, that if the other countries did not make some concession the Americans should threaten to leave. In order to be prepared for such a move, he cabled back to the United States to learn how soon a ship could be sent to France, possibly intending to use its presence to back up such a threat. Fortunately, in the next few days concessions were made. The problem of the Saar was settled by letting France exploit it for the next fifteen years. The men at the peace congress had acted like children. If the game was not played so they could win, they refused to play. A short time later the Italians did leave in protest against the way in which Wilson refused their demands.

A third sore spot was Shantung. Shantung was a province on the coast of China that was as dear to the hearts of the Chinese as Mount Vernon is to Americans. Before the war it had been taken from China by Germany in retaliation for the murder of some German missionaries. During the war Japan had insisted upon coming to the aid of Great Britain, in spite of British protests, and "helped the British" by taking Shantung from the Germans, that is, from China. Japan insisted upon being allowed to keep the province after the war, and used four arguments so influential that even Wilson agreed. According to his policy of self-determination of nations, Shantung belonged to China if anything belonged to anybody. The Japanese said they had a treaty with China, signed the year before, granting them the right to occupy Shantung, but omitted to say that the treaty was signed at the point of a gun. They insisted that the Allies had no right to make them give up Shantung unless France and Great Britain also gave up the portions of China which they held. They resorted to bargaining power by suggesting that a clause on racial equality should be included in the covenant of the League, knowing that the United States Senate would never consent to such a League. They didn't want the clause, but it was a good way to scare Wilson. Finally they threatened to go home; and since the Italians had already left, this was no idle threat. It might mean the collapse of the congress. Wilson had to choose between giving the Japanese the booty they demanded so unscrupulously and the probability of seeing his whole plan of a world settlement scuttled. He chose to give Shantung to the Japanese. To blame him would be unfair until some solution can be offered for the triple problem of national boundaries.

The three cases just cited are not merely past history. They cannot be forgotten like a bad dream while we fabricate plans *de novo* for the postwar world. They are still sore spots. These and many other actual problems just like them will have to be settled before there can be any permanent world peace. Most important of all, some formula must be found for solving the fundamental difficulty of boundaries.

The most famous plan adopted by the Congress of Paris for rebuilding the world was, secondly, the League of Nations. The congress had to choose between two types of world union, voluntary and involuntary. A voluntary union would be one which nations would join of their own choice, to which they would contribute as they pleased, and from which they could withdraw at any time. This, strictly speaking, is a league of nations. The involuntary union would be one which nations would be forced to join; which would compel them to pay taxes, obey laws, and submit to supervision; and which would never allow them to secede. This is essentially a world state. Wilson insisted upon having a voluntary league, for the very good reason that it would have been folly to have expected the United States to agree to a world state, and he desired a league rather than nothing.

Although the League of Nations as established by the Treaty of Versailles accomplished many improvements in world civilization, as a world union it failed. For that failure there are three chief reasons. The first was its purpose. The League was intended to rectify the errors of the peace treaty Wilson was wise enough to realize that any treaty made in so short a time, under such adverse circumstances, must contain weaknesses, such as the settlement of the Shantung question. However, he hoped that, if the treaty could be completed and the League actually put into operation, the League itself would iron out the mistakes. Unfortunately, the League was unequal to its mission. It failed to carry through the program for disarmament of the world which was laid upon it as a primary obligation. It allowed the weak to be plundered

16

by the strong. Not being good enough for the supreme tasks laid upon it, it was rejected as good for nothing.

A second reason for its collapse was peace. Contrary to popular imagination, peace is not an ending of all troubles. It brings with it new and difficult problems. One of these problems is that it removes the bond of unity that holds allies together, namely, the common danger. It is historically unnatural for countries that have fought together against a common foe to keep working together in time of peace.

A third reason was that each nation valued the League in accordance with its own self-interest. The nations supported the League for what it could give them and not for its own sake. Its councils at Geneva needed the support of a spirit of world loyalty, and this support they never had. In this respect the attitude of the United States was not different in kind from that of other nations. Without world-mindedness any league was doomed from the start. And world-mindedness was a hopeless dream, because any leader who placed the interests of the world above those of the nation that put him in office was sure to lose its support. It is not strange, therefore, that during this second World War postwar planning has shifted its hopes from a voluntary league to an involuntary world state.

The silences of Versailles were a negative part of its rebuilding program. The treaty deliberately ignored many problems of reconstruction because the congress thought it was good policy to ignore them. This was a fatal mistake. Trends in world development cannot be silenced by being ignored; they must be faced squarely. Two of these trends will certainly face the peacemakers at the end of this conflict, even as they faced the pacifiers of Paris. One is communism, the movement of the proletariat to establish a dictatorship of their class by a world revolution. Communism was a menace to world peace in 1919; it was one of the chief causes of this war; and it must be dealt with vigorously or it will cause

17

further bloodshed. A second trend was the danger of a post-war depression. On this the Treaty of Versailles was sadly silent. Wars are almost invariably followed by hard times due largely to the war. This war will be no exception. The Versailles Treaty could have made at least an effort to ward off the depression. It did nothing, and the depression proved disastrous for world peace.

IV. ENDING THE WAR

A fourth difficulty confronting any group of peacemakers is the task of ending the war—that is, stopping the fighting, sending the soldiers home, and replacing military action by friendly relations between nations. In solving this problem the Congress of Paris made a dismal failure.

It is a common misconception that Germany surrendered unconditionally. The armistice terms, it is true, did stipulate unconditional surrender; but the Allies were bound by their own commitments to respect certain promises to the world. Wilson's Fourteen Points were intended to be regarded by the German people as a favorable program by which they would be treated, and so to induce them to yield. On November 5, 1918, the Fourteen Points were supplemented by a statement, called the Pre-Armistice Agreements, which stated definitely how the Allies would act on certain matters in case of a German surrender. The German people might even have gained the impression that, if they overthrew the Kaiser and his gang of militarists, Germany would be treated as a country that had taken the first step on the road to reform and needed to be encouraged.

It was no encouragement to reform, however, when Germany was not allowed to send envoys to the peace congress. Only toward the end of the congress, after the peace was practically completed, were German delegates summoned to appear; and then they were kept in virtual imprisonment at Versailles while the treaty was submitted to them for their perusal. They were allowed to submit their criticisms in writing, but only a few objections were heeded. Germany was treated like a guilty nation that couldn't be trusted. The terms of the treaty were so rigorous that the head of the German commission resigned rather than sign it, and only the threat of renewed war induced the other German delegates to place their signatures on the document. Thus they condemned themselves to eternal disgrace in the eyes of their countrymen.

The signing of the treaty took place, not at Paris, where it had been drafted, but at Versailles. There were plenty of elegant tables at Paris and a full supply of ink. Why, then, this pilgrimage to a mildewed palace in the country? There was a reason, a good reason, which every Frenchman and every German understood only too well. Versailles had been built by Louis XIV, the king who was chiefly responsible for taking from Germany the territory between the Saône and the Rhine. Versailles was the place where France had paid for that "crime" on January 18, 1871. That was the day on which the triumphant armies of Bismarck brought William the First to the Hall of Mirrors to be crowned Emperor of the German Empire over the prostrate body of France. Now the Germans were in turn forced to "eat dirt" in the same place where they had triumphed so arrogantly. The signing of the treaty at Versailles was intended as a deliberate insult to Germany, an insult that wiped out the hurt to French pride.

The terms of the treaty were extremely severe. It contained a long list of German "crimes," not for just the past four years of war. This arraignment went back a century and a half to the theft of West Prussia from Poland in 1772. The notorious "war guilt clause" placed upon Germany the full responsibility for the war. The German colonies were taken away. Alsace and Lorraine were returned to France. To the average American that seemed only common justice, but not so to Germany. There were plenty of people in Alsace who spoke German. Their ancestors were German, and some of them preferred to go into voluntary exile rather than stay under French rule. Germany was disarmed and reduced to the rank of a third-rate power in military might. The Rhineland, the beautiful region which every German loved as much as his own home, was occupied by foreign troops, some of them Negroes from Africa. And even this fell far short of French desires; for France had demanded that a Rhineland republic should be established, dominated by France and used as a buffer state against Germany. Probably the most serious blow was the imposition of reparations, a program so far-reaching in its results that it will be given fuller discussion below.

The brutal and atrocious way in which Germany waged the war is such common knowledge that it would be foolish to attempt to excuse it, and it certainly is not the purpose of this lecture to do so. Neither is it the intention of this author to join any indiscriminate condemnation of the "injustices of Versailles." Compared with the great treaties of history, it was the equal of any of them in effort and wisdom. Nevertheless, any impartial appraisal of the treaty cannot avoid the evident conclusion that this was not a treaty of peace; it was a treaty of war. This was not a program of reform for Germany; it was condemnation to life imprisonment. It did not end the war; it only changed its form. Future peacemakers must make a decision between punishment of the enemy or peace with the enemy. This the Treaty of Versailles failed to do.

V. Preserving the Peace

Every truly successful peace treaty must not only end the war but also include measures to keep the treaty in operation so that future discord may not develop into armed strife. This is the task of preserving peace. The Treaty of Versailles included several provisions intended to achieve this end; but they all failed, either because they were inadequate or because they were handicapped by other provisions. The feature that

20

was chiefly responsible for undermining the peace was the reparations program. A study of this one error alone is sufficient to explain why the peace was not preserved, although of course there were many other reasons.

The Pre-Armistice Agreements had stated that Germany would be expected to pay "for all the damage done to the civilian population of the Allies and their property." In other words, Germany was expected to pay the repair bill. Within a month, however, the situation had changed. In the first part of December an election for a new parliament was held in Great Britain, known to history as the Khaki Election. During the campaign there was a vigorous demand in England that Germany should be made to pay the full costs of the war. Lloyd George, the prime minister, wanted to stay in office. If he was to win the peace, he must first win the election. He realized that Germany could only get the means to pay by selling abroad, and that she couldn't sell abroad to any extent without selling where the British wanted to sell. But this argument, sound as it was, would not get votes. So, in order to get the votes, Lloyd George compromised by saying that he would demand full war costs at the peace congress. At the same time he also said that he thought it was an impossible demand, but he didn't say this so loud. He won the election.

The result was a conflict at Paris between the Americans, who backed the repair bill policy, and the British, who demanded some kind of war costs. After prolonged discussion a compromise was proposed by one of the American delegates. He suggested that a statement should be included in the treaty that Germany ought to pay full war costs, but would be asked to pay only civilian damages. The result was the famous war-guilt clause placing all the blame for the war upon Germany:

The Allied and Associated Governments affirm, and Germany accepts, the responsibility of Germany and her allies for causing all the loss and damage to which the Allied and Associated Governments and their nationals have been subjected as a consequence of the war imposed upon them by the aggression of Germany and her allies.

The statement was historically untrue. For example, there is good evidence that the murder of the Archduke, which started the war, was plotted by Serbia. The war-guilt clause did lots of harm and little good, for it gave Germany a strong argument for saying that the whole treaty was unjust and that any punishment based upon this accusation should be resisted. True or untrue, its psychological effect in Germany was disastrous for preserving peace.

Near the end of the congress Wilson was finally persuaded by the British, contrary to the advice of the Americans, that pensions and dependence allowances should be included in civilian damages. Such sophistry was not calculated to gain a reputation of justice for the peace treaty.

After months of bickering the peace congress was still unable to decide how much Germany should be asked to pay, and how long she should be given to pay it; so a temporary plan was adopted. According to this, Germany was to pay about five billion dollars. In the meantime a reparations commission would work out a permanent settlement. After about two years the permanent plan was finished. By then Germany had paid, according to her own claim, the full five billion; but the Allies asserted that the total value of her payments, in money and goods, was less than half that amount. The result was that both sides accused each other of insincerity and foul play.

The permanent plan called for the payment of about thirty-two billion dollars in sixty years, at the rate of one-half billion a year plus interest. Germany claimed that this was a fantastic amount and offered to pay about eight billion. The Allies threatened war; and Germany accepted their ultimatum to pay or else, and signed the agreement on May 11, 1921.

The result was failure. The first installment was paid on time. Then Germany pleaded poverty and won first a postponement and then smaller payments. Finally she stopped paying altogether after a little more than a year.

Meanwhile German paper currency had fallen far below its prewar value and was destined to fall so low it was valueless. Perhaps this was due to manipulation by a government that wanted to create an excuse for not paying. Probably Germany did cheat and stall on the reparations payments. Nevertheless the significant fact for the preserving of the peace was that there was tremendous suffering in Germany. The middle class saw their earnings and savings almost completely wiped out of existence. If there were any "reformers" in the "Fatherland" who wanted to co-operate with the program of peace, they had little reason to place their confidence in the makers of the reparations arrangement.

The French, in spite of British objections, sent an army into the rich manufacturing district of the Ruhr Valley to force the Germans to disgorge some money. The invasion was a failure. By the end of 1923 the reparations program had completely collapsed.

However, France, Great Britain, and the other Allies could not afford to let reparations go by the board. They had borrowed about ten billion dollars from the United States, counting on the reparations from Germany to provide the money to repay it. Now they changed their policy. Instead of continuing the reparations war, for that is what it really was, they decided to treat this as a business proposition. They called in business experts, and under the leadership of Charles E. Dawes these experts drew up the Dawes Plan. Economically the plan was sound. It provided for a large loan to Germany on the basis of which German business could recover itself. Reparations payments were to be renewed with a first payment of about one-quarter of a billion. In the following four years the payments gradually increased to three-quarters of a billion

23

dollars. There were only two serious weaknesses in the arrangement. It made no estimate of the total bill for Germany, and it provided for only five years of payments.

Under the operation of the Dawes Plan the next five years appeared to be a period of stabilization and reform for Germany. German currency was restored to a firm basis. Germany joined the League of Nations. The Locarno Treaties were signed, accepting the Rhine boundary. The Paris Peace Pact renouncing war was adopted by Germany. Apparently the Reich was once more a respectable member of the family of nations. Unfortunately, much of this improvement was not only superficial but deceptive. While business appeared to prosper, the amount of German debts increased. The middle class which had been ruined by the postwar depression of 1919-23, failed to recover and looked around desperately for a deliverer.

In 1929 the five-year arrangement of the Dawes Plan expired. To provide a permanent settlement, the Young Plan was drafted after months of labor by a committee of experts headed by Owen D. Young. At the beginning of June, 1929, the plan was announced to the world with a tremendous fanfare of favorable publicity. It has generally been regarded as a marvelous achievement. However, this opinion is open to question. Instead of being a solution of the reparations problem, it actually proved to be the turn in the tide away from the preserving of peace toward the next war. Though its designers no doubt had the best of intentions, the Young Plan had four disastrous features from a political point of view. First, it reduced the total amount that Germany had to pay to about eight billion dollars, approximately what Germany had first offered to pay. But the interest charges increased this amount to almost the sum which Germany still had to pay without interest under the first plan. It was still large enough to appear impossible. Second, it provided for payment by a series of installments that were both small and adjustable;

but each payment was based upon the presumption of German war guilt. Each and every payment was a tacit admission by Germany of a charge that was galling to the German soul. For two generations this was to go on so that the children's children would pay for the sins of their fathers. Third, the total amount, as well as the size of the payments was almost the same as the payments owed by the Allies to the United States. And Germany was told that if the United States agreed to take less from the Allies, then the Allies would demand less from Germany. In other words, the Allies were collecting money to hand over to the "rich and greedy" Americans. Thus *they* had little to gain from reparations. Why, then, should they exert themselves to force Germany to pay? Fourth, all guarantees, such as the occupation of the Rhineland, were removed. To remove guarantees at the very time when the Germans were already convinced that they ought not to pay was a strange procedure. If guarantees ever were needed, it was then.

After much opposition Great Britain signed the Young Plan on August 28, 1929. But it took almost a year to overcome German opposition and get the scheme into operation. On October 24, 1929, only two months after the Young Plan was adopted, the Wall Street crash started a world depression that spread to Europe. In May, 1931, the largest bank in Vienna crashed. Soon afterwards Germany stopped payments on reparations. The Hoover moratorium in the next month only made matters worse. On the other side of the world Japan read the signs of the times. The nations were too deeply involved with their economic troubles to interfere with her; so she embarked on a career of conquest by attacking Mukden, in China, September 18, 1931. That was the real beginning of the second World War. Two years later the German people, disillusioned by the Young Plan and discouraged by the depression, put their destinies into the hands of Adolf Hitler. From that time on there was no possible chance of preserving the peace.

It is not the purpose of this record either to justify or to condemn German actions. Its purpose is to explain why the nation of Germany acted as it did. Only by such an explanation can it be made clear that it is not enough to make postwar plans; they must be good plans.

While nobody can foresee the future, there is every reason to believe that the same five difficulties that spelled disaster for the Treaty of Versailles will confront the world at the end of this war. Any postwar planning that leaves these difficulties unanswered is largely idle talk. These main problems must be solved first, or they will cause the fall of the whole structure and war will break out again.

POWER POLITICS AND THE POSTWAR WORLD

ROBERT S. LYND

Professor of Sociology, Columbia University

WHAT I SAY HERE WILL TROUBLE SOME, PERHAPS MANY; and I believe it should. For the thing I shall discuss is the wide, and I believe disastrous, gap that exists between what the decent people of the democracies are wanting and hoping and what the pressure of circumstances and organized power under the surface in democracy may force upon us.

I spent three months this summer crisscrossing endlessly up and down Britain speaking on the United States under our Office of War Information and the British Ministry of Information. I spoke to middle-class men and women, workers in their canteens, social clubs and trade unions, men in the armed forces, fire-watching groups, and the men and women of the superb National Fire Service. They are a tremendously decent folk—tired, living in real danger, doing without things to a degree hard for us to realize over here, and yet with a twinkle in the eye and even a good-natured wisecrack. They are a people hoping, just as we do over here, that something really better will come out of this war. Always, I felt the basic likeness between those decent, hopeful people, the middle-class and working-class people of Britain, and us ordinary folk of America.

Their orientation toward the future is a nip more realistic than ours, as it should be with the English Channel shrunken as an effective frontier to the width of one of our Midwestern creeks. I talked with hundreds of our American soldiers on trains and in the streets. England hadn't changed them. They still talked like our people here at home, and I had the fol-

27

lowing sense of difference between the English outlook on the future and that of us Americans: The people of both nations hope vaguely or concretely for a better world in general, but they differ in their expectations of fundamental change within their own respective nations. The mood of our people is, as I sense it, like that of a man who has been driving along a broad concrete road at fifty miles an hour and has come to a barrier marked "Detour—Road under Repair"; so he is now, during the war, bumping along at fifteen miles an hour in the field beside the road; but he takes it for granted that right up there behind that clump of trees he'll be back on the concrete again. In England, on the other hand, as they bump along over the rough war road, everybody takes it for granted that there will be extensive new road-building ahead. But I felt in England, as I feel here, a basic unpreparedness and helplessness of the ordinary folk to implement their hopes, and the strong likelihood that, as I have just said, the pressure of circumstances—that is, the need for swift, effective action and the pressure of organized power groups—will force upon them concurrence in a world they never intended.

I am skeptical of the great plans of liberal intellectuals for a brave new world out of this war, and of the hopes of our citizens that so readily leap after these plans. And I say this as one committed to the need to use intelligence to implement our values, and committed to the necessity for hoping and implementing our hoping by working. But I am skeptical because I believe that democracy is woefully unprepared and, especially, unorganized to state its program positively and to see that democratic program through by organized action. I believe that it is now 11:59 P.M. and that events have an accumulated momentum which probably cannot be stopped or even seriously deflected in this final minute of feverish effort. Caught in this critical moment of time, our thinking as regards these great liberal plans is omitting, I believe, some crucial intermediate steps.

It makes no sense simply to dismiss such a point of view as

28

"defeatist." That is one of the cheap clichés of the day. Both "optimist" and "defeatist" are lazy attitudes and lazy epithets. As currently used, they do not fit the citizen who is committed all-out to democracy, who believes it will win out over the long pull, who is working for it, but who sees trouble in the years immediately ahead and refuses to play ostrich.

What is this future that looks to me so dangerously coercive?

Nobody can know the future with assurance. We differ in our interest in and ability to grasp the future. As regards our difference in interest, some of us would rather not know what is coming, would rather just wait and face it when it comes—particularly if the future is to be bad news! As regards ability to grasp present tendencies that will spell themselves out as the future, H. N. Brailsford, the veteran British publicist, has said that "men differ in their perceptive capacity chiefly in their ability to see movement." So one gropes and cannot be sure, but I believe one does not grope entirely in the dark.

As I try to appraise the lines of movement from today to the last half of the 1940's, here are the guiding assumptions I make:

1. One may not expect new and better things of the postwar world merely because men of good will all over the world are fed up with war, depression and unemployment, aggressive nationalism, and fascism.

2. The future will be primarily determined by the nature and manner of operation of the institutions that have been in operation before and during the last war and in the 1920's and 1930's, and that are in operation in the manner of fighting this war.

3. The operation of institutional systems depends primarily upon who has power—not theoretical power but factual power to do decisive things.

4. The power policies of groups and classes holding power tend simply to do more of the same, that is, to continue along

29

the line they have been following, unless and to the extent that internal difficulty within the system or coercion from rival national systems proves sufficiently serious to force some adaptation; and in that event these adaptations tend only to be either an intensification of power tactics to beat down the opposition or the least possible adaptations calculated to keep the going system running.

It becomes crucially important, therefore, to ask: Who, factually, hold power in current institutional systems? And what are those holding power after? And, since institutional power systems are dynamic, that is, have momentum in operation, where are the points at which there simply are no options at present, but only stark institutional coercions? And where, within the broad coercions of this dynamic system, do points of option really lie?

What I am trying to do is to pull our focus down from the big schemes for an international rule of reason under international agreement and formal law to considerations less glamorous, and closer to home: to such things as the going structure of power within the nations that would be asked to enter such international agreements. Plans like Mr. Culbertson's for an international police force need to be drafted and discussed, and I am for them. But does Mr. Culbertson really expect a hard-pressed Britain after this war to allow and to support an international agency that controls what Britain may and may not do, in her desperate need to re-establish her economic base in world trade by hook or by crook? Likewise, Mr. Lippmann's *U. S. Foreign Policy* is an admirable and important book. But it omits half the picture in concentrating as it does on sovereign states as though they were unified things with only their sovereignty as governments to consider. And it fails to give due weight to the strength and international character of modern capitalism, to the power of national economies in controlling state policy, and to the ultimate significance of ideologies in the relations of the United States and the Soviet Union, and of the

Vatican and the Soviet Union. The explosive relief that greeted the Teheran agreement, with its promises of international comity, vaulted easily over the web of underlying critical issues, although these are precisely the kinds of issues that rise up to defeat every attempt at solution of major international problems by formal agreements among sovereign states. *Business Week* asks succinctly of such an agreement: "Will a free economy [the United States] be put at a disadvantage by close political ties with two countries, one [Soviet Russia] with an absolutely controlled economy, the other [Britain] with an economy that will have to be increasingly controlled to insure survival?" That is the sort of question that suggests where the international shoe may rub the national foot.

Here is the same ultimate difficulty that besets the plans for planned economies of men like Keynes and Hansen—always this crucial political problem of power. One can now say with assurance that the problems that bar the way to effective national economic planning are *not* economic. We know what to do in the economic sphere. But the critical problem, the "stumper," is the political problem: Will those who hold power in the economic sphere surrender their arbitrary power and co-operate with the planners?

So what I am doing is not belittling plans for a new world of international co-operation, the outlawing of war, and so on. I am simply saying that, before we let our hopes soar with these plans, we would better take a good look at the operations of the armament industries between the two wars as revealed in the Nye committee report. That situation has not changed. We would better look at the record of business in World War I, as revealed, for instance, in chapters 9-13 of Carl Dreher's *The Coming Showdown*. That situation has not changed. We would better look at business feathering its nest with unparalleled profits in this war; at big business fighting off the needed use of little business by crippling the Small War Plants Corporation; and at our democratic government being forced largely to fight this present war on big business' own terms.

Let's look at this problem of power in industrial society as revealed in the case of the United States. What is our American theory of power? As a democracy we have believed that power should be diffused among all adult citizens. The state has no independent power but holds its power from the citizens. Power has been regarded as pluralistic: to the kind of power that the state represents we have applied the adjective "political," while other kinds of power—social power and notably economic power—we have regarded as each a separate thing apart from "political" power, and as things that political power can always reach out and curb whenever occasion raises. Taken as a whole, this is an essentially naïve theory of power.

Latent within the American attempt to marry political democracy and private capitalism was a major conflict between majority rule and minority property rights. And the sophisticates among the Founding Fathers were aware of it. The preponderant weight of economic power in the Constitutional Convention, while conceding the outward forms of political democracy, went on to cripple democratic power at the source by parceling up this power by a marvelously dexterous system of barriers to its expression. And political power was diffused among the people on the unstated, but factually double-locked, assumption that it was not to be used to diffuse equality in the economic sphere.

Actually, our nation was founded in a backswing of revulsion from centralized power. Such power was viewed as a thing to be feared, not used. The problem of power was stated negatively. And our political democracy has, all down through our national life, been casual to the point of recklessness about the positive development of its own authority. Formally, the democratic state has held all the aces; but actually as time has passed, to use Harold Laski's words, "The disproportion in America between the actual economic control and the formal political power is almost fantastic."

Despite intermittent guerilla skirmishes between state power and private economic power, for example, under the antitrust laws, American democracy has been sluggish about recognizing the challenge to its very existence inherent in growing economic power. Several factors have encouraged this casual attitude within democracy:

1. The fact that the issue between democratic power and private economic power has been so heavily cloaked under the sectional issue between agragrian and eastern industrial states has diverted attention from the fact that capitalist economic power constitutes a direct, continuous, and fundamental threat to the whole structure of democratic authority everywhere and always.

2. Again, the fact that American democracy began coincidentally with the amazing productive advance we call the industrial revolution and the opportunity to exploit the vast internal empire of the United States made it easy for the citizens of democracy to take democracy for granted as essentially completed, whereas they had made only a beginning at building democracy. They turned their back on democracy's unfinished business and plunged into the grand personal adventure of growing rich. In this burgeoning young society the reigning attitude has been: "Why worry? We can face problems as they come up." The only trouble has been that we have not faced this problem of power squarely.

3. The "American way"—loose-jointed, wasteful, evoking prodigies of energy from men in the raw frontier era of pre-empt and exploit—has yielded a sumptuous "take." And, as a nation manifestly growing rich, the growing insecurities within such a predatory institutional system have prompted us to seek security, not through re-examining that system and its contradictions, but through the simpler process of reaffirming the perfection and finality of the Constitution. We have regarded a formal document, instead of the living tissue of democracy, as our guarantee.

33

Such has been the theory of power held by us hopeful and busy Americans. But what is the fact of power in industrial society today?

1. Power is indivisible, and economic power *is* political power. The effort to view political power and economic power as separate things is, has been, and always will be a fiction. This integral nature of power has been concealed in the democratic state by the illusion that the state represents the common interests of the people. But, as Monograph 26 of the Senate Temporary National Economic Committee dealing with *Economic Power and Political Pressures* reveals, the geographical basis of our legislative representation "obscures the economic or functional basis for legislative decisions"; and, with a few major exceptions, congressmen "appear to respond more readily to pressure from business than from other groups. . . . Pressure groups generally find it more satisfactory to influence the votes of legislators in their behalf than to try to elect their own representatives to office." And "the role of the general public in the contest [for power] may to a large extent be ignored, since the public is generally too formless, too inchoate, to apply pressure at given points for a given purpose, and is largely the passive instrument which both business and government use to strengthen their own arms."

In connection with this last point concerning the weak role of the general public, let me stress the fact that power means effective power, and effective power in modern society means organized power. A crucial problem democracy faces today is its lack of effective organization to carry on its affairs. We have proceeded, all down through our national life, on the casual assumption that men are rational and free; that they know what is best for them; and that, therefore, no positive philosophy of social organization is needed, because men can be counted on to recognize the need for organizing themselves wherever that need exists and to go ahead and organize themselves. The catch here is that this assumption about human behavior just isn't true. And, as a result, the social organization of the United States today is a shambles, characterized by grossly uneven organization, with business and industry increasingly extensively and effectively organized, with labor rising in organization to meet organized business, and with organization behind other interests of the people of democracy lamentably weak and spotty. This, I submit, is a design for democratic impotence. With no positive policy for democratic organization, and with such spotty and ineffectual organization in behalf of many phases of the public interest of democracy, those interest areas where extensive and effective organization exists tend to define for democracy the public interest, and to define it in terms of their own private interests. And the power of the meagerly organized or unorganized people of democracy tends to become chiefly the power to protest raggedly after the fact, after a *fait accompli*, like a man futilely running after the ever-receding rear platform of a train.

2. A second important aspect of power in industrial society today is its technological base. Power in earlier eras was founded on land; later it was based on finance, the control of free capital; but today the basis of power is control over technology. By this I do not mean what James Burnham means in his *Managerial Revolution;* for it simply is not true that "managers" are neutral as regards power and are not controlled by business power. But what I mean is that the business system of power that controls giant technology controls the core of power in industrial society. Look at the way big industry has moved in on the government in this war and is coercing the government to run the war effort as business itself dictates. Or turn again to the same monograph of the Senate's study of the concentration of economic power I cited previously. On page 22 it says, "The control over applied science which business holds is the key to the explanation of its dominant position in the process of government. . . . By its control over technology it is able to perpetu-

ate that position." So, I say, technology—its efficiency, its plans, and its requirements in the way of markets—controls today the wealth of nations and nations' political policies. And this brings me to the final aspect of the fact of power in contemporary industrial society that I want to stress.

3. The central political fact in the world today is the candid merging of state power with this technologically based economic power. The day is past, forever, when a nation could afford to view what businessmen do as primarily only the concern of businessmen. A state-sponsored industrial Germany, starting late in its quest for world markets, began to overtake England, with the latter's economic liberalism and comfortable head start at industrialization, in the 1870's. And the decade of the 1880's may be viewed as the turning point at which Britain began frankly to forsake a governmental policy of *laissez faire*. In World War I industrial Germany made her first formal bid for an enlarged world for her machines. And the fundamental import of what has been happening at a quickening tempo since the Russian Revolution of 1917 has been the abandonment of the liberal fiction that private business is not public business. Within a world of shrunken time and space and of chronic technological over-capacity, the coercions of capitalist competition are increasing sharply. And to nations that have experienced the gigantic costs of mass unemployment, the possibility of full employment, and therefore the necessity for achieving relatively full employment, these coercions are no longer matters that may be disregarded. In the United States, for instance, operating under private capitalism and with fourteen billion dollars of new wartime productive plant—superefficient and built for mass production—the structure of our industry has been seriously altered by the war; and foreign trade in greater volume and variety will be an absolute essential for even approximate economic stability. And if we are in this box, I need not elaborate how desperate is Britain's

need to crowd the tradeways of the world with her products —to the fighting limit.

What this sort of thing means, in nation after nation, is that business, on the one hand, is less and less willing and able to tolerate checks on its activities by the state; whereas the state, on the other hand, having delivered its welfare, and fundamentally its international power, over into dependence upon the welfare of its business system, needs increasingly the utmost efficiency from its businessmen. So, from here on out, business must be in politics and the state must be in business. Neither of them can any longer tolerate the frictions and inefficiencies of the kind of legalized guerilla warfare between state apparatus and economic apparatus that has been characteristic of antitrust actions, New Deal antagonisms, and wartime coercions and recriminations. And the resulting trend is unmistakably toward the monolithic power structure of the totalitarian state. Not, mark you, because certain men are wicked or even necessarily see as yet that they are being forced toward such totalitarianism. In fact, current business advertisements call insistently for the return to free enterprise. But the trend is against this because the logic of giant technology, operating within nationalism and capitalist rules of the game, no longer allows any other option than centralization and the merging of state and economic power. We people who talk of a better postwar world must face, and face unflinchingly, the fact which liberal democracy has never dared really to face: namely, that industrial capitalism in an era of giant technology is an intensively coercive form of organization of society that cumulatively constrains men and all of their institutions to work the will of the minority who hold and wield economic power; and that this relentless warping of men's lives and decisions and all of their forms of association becomes less and less the result of voluntary decisions by "good" and "bad" men and more and more an impersonal web of coercions dictated by the stark need to keep "the system" going.

37

What this means is that Hitlers are not themselves prime causes but are a type of role thrust forward by the pressure of events within industrial society, events demanding solutions —political solutions, bold solutions, solutions that brush intellectuals and the plans of decent men aside like flies off a table. And when big industrialists buy a Hitler into power to break the back of rising organized demands by labor and thereby to facilitate national competitive advantage; or when, working through ministry officers, they deliberately stall and sabotage a humanly decent and needed thing like the Beveridge Plan or all postwar social planning, as is the case in Britain today; or when they go all-out, as our National Association of Manufacturers is doing, in frightening and capturing well-meaning citizens, their educators, the ministers in their churches, in the drive to defeat progressive New Deal legislation—when these things happen, they are not the work of evil men but, rather, the grim moves of hard-pressed players in the gigantic international poker game in which each industry and nation must play to survive.

Modern war, as a mass human experience, does a variety of contrasting things to us:

1. It is a time of enormously enhanced pressure, pressure to get things—even things that seem impossible under peacetime institutions—done and done immediately. And since the game is for keeps and the stakes are survival, there is a tendency to create and foster a temporary and somewhat "phony" sense of national unity, and a tendency to disregard, in the intensity of short-run wartime preoccupations, the chronic and deep cleavages within American or English society. So one thing war tends to do is temporarily to dull our critical sense and to give us a specious sense of social solidarity. When that is in time shown up for what it is, it tends to be followed by social cynicism. We have heard much of the new classless Britain born in the heroic times of Dunkerque and the Battle of Britain. But, with victory in sight, the old Britain is

again returned—class system, Tory power, and all. And people wince when they admit this in England today.

2. At the same time war also does a seemingly contradictory thing. By shattering the lock-step preoccupation with habitual institutional ways of doing things, it invites some men to speculate as regards new goals and a better world. Humble men's imaginations in England have been caught and aroused by the vision of Russia as a nation in which people are being allowed to fight this war "all out." As the London *Economist* says, ". . . the passion for Russia that has been such a feature of the last two years is probably to be interpreted . . . as . . . envy of a country that is not frustrated." Likewise, some intellectuals turn afresh, under the stimulus of war, to the development of plans for international co-operation. Thus war, instead of merely encouraging the glossing over of social problems can also jolt and stimulate men of all classes to reach for new goals and to chart novel courses toward them.

3. But let's not deceive ourselves. War does still another thing. Common folk dream their hopes and intellectuals spin their plans, yet still other men are learning other things from this war. Big business controllers of industry are perceiving their terrible jeopardy in the postwar world; and they are getting a dress rehearsal in organized power tactics free from the constraints of antitrust and other serious governmental controls. As big business looks ahead at the probable raw, bare-fisted battle-royal for world trade and economic survival in the postwar world, it is learning the vast profitableness of a business world that largely staffs the government with its own men, that has the brass hats of the armed forces as its ally, and that so largely runs the nation on its own terms. Big business will emerge from this war enormously better organized, more sure of the direction it must go, and more powerful than ever before. That goes for the United States. And it goes for Britain. And business is not spending time spinning pretty humanitarian plans for a League

of Nations and an international police force. The sort of plans it is making may be seen in *The National Policy for Industry*, put out by 120 British industrialists in November, 1942. Faith in the power of humanitarian reason to transcend stark interest isn't going to stop powerhouse tactics like those.

As I appraise the situation that has industrial society (you and me) and its institutions in its grip, the technological pressure toward centralized control is so great as to be inevitable; and that means that the movement toward national economic planning in each industrial nation is inevitable. The current debate as to whether to plan or not plan is today as unreal as would have been the debate in 1800 as to whether to use or not use power-driven machinery. Here, in this question as to whether to move toward centralization and national planning, there is literally no longer any option. The only remaining option—and a desperate one for democracy in its present poorly organized state—is *whether organized economic power will take over state power and run the nation primarily for the goals of big business under an American and British version of fascism, or whether the democratic state will take over the economy, socialize it, and run it for the welfare of the mass of the people.*

So there is a war within the war going on inside each nation living under capitalism. And the Catholic Church, the greatest organized private power in the world next to big business, is predominantly on the side of capitalist economic power. It is this "war within the war" that was responsible for the shabby role of the United States and England as regards Loyalist Spain; for the Darlan and Peyroutan shuffling in North Africa; for the disreputable fumbling with Badoglio and the King in Italy, whereby, as one bold critic in the House of Commons phrased it, "The Allied High Command have approached the Italian mainland like an old man approaching a young bride—fascinated, sluggish, and apprehensive." And it is this "war within the war" that leaves the German people cowering united under our bombs because we have offered them no wholehearted alternative to Vansit-tartism.

We live in one of the climactic eras of history, as crucial as the revolutionary era of one hundred and fifty years ago. And it is characteristic of such a time that it is a time of extreme ideological confusion. Fascist monopolistic capitalism calls itself "national socialism." Russian socialism still hangs in the balance, apparently a largely socialist-aimed economy within a dictatorship by the Communist Party. Whether the Soviet Union will after this war renew, with the new confidence in itself and its institutions won in the magnificent people's effort of its Stalingrads, the march toward democracy promised in the New Constitution of the mid-1930's remains to be seen. I profoundly hope so. Here in the United States, again a manifestation of this ideological confusion, organized industry opposes organized labor in the name of "democracy." And characteristic of this confusion is the fact that we Americans tend to identify democracy and capitalistic free enterprise as two aspects of the same thing—a disastrously naïve belief! For the world issue today, the thing Hitlers stand for, is a counter-revolution against democracy. And, again characteristic of the world-wide ideological confusion, the men who in a country like the United States coerce democracy in the name of "free enterprise" do so not as cynical Macchiavellis but as men who, for the most part, honestly believe in democracy.

I am afraid that we people of democracy are going to come out of this war with our democratic ideals badly soiled, and well on the road to less democracy here at home. I don't believe that, either in England or the United States, the soldiers will return prepared to fight positively for democracy. The mood of soldiers and civilians at war's weary end will be: "Thank God! Now let's get out the old car and begin to live again!" Both among soldiers and civilians this relaxed mood of war's end will present a powerful weapon to the forces of reaction. In England, Winston Churchill's history of World War I shows clearly that, as a Tory, he grasped

41

the political significance of the mood of popular relaxation that followed November 11, 1918. And it is no accident that today he is consistently fighting off social reform during the war, thereby postponing the issue to the time when it will be no unmanageable one. For, during that period of rejoicing when the public ceases momentarily to care for anything but the fact that the fighting has ceased, Tory power will quietly gather up the reins and commence the drive to hold its power. And that in a country where there is an organized Labour Party and where men can call themselves "socialists" without lowering their voices! So the signals seem set for an exhausted peace dictated by power.

I have suggested that this present moment in time is 11:59 P.M. You and I and the democracy we believe in are probably due for defeat in this round. But the hands of the clock will move on! What have we learned? What must we learn from the frustration of this second and more disastrous great war in our lifetime? I believe this:

1. Democracy's cause cannot be won by applying rational rules to international society if the internal war within capitalist nations is left unwon by democracy.

2. So the test of the *bona fides* of our current thinking about a better world is whether it includes plans for immediate and fundamental extension of democracy to our internal American economic institutions.

3. Lazy democratic citizenship that comes up for air to vote only once every four years can never curb an economic power that is organized and working all the time.

I believe profoundly in the eventual victory of democracy —over the long future. But the road back will be long, and American democracy carries no lucky horseshoe in its pocket. A recent issue of the London *Economist* says, "Democracy in the twentieth century needs fire in its belly." And, let me add, only organization, grass-roots organization, pervasive organization of all of us in the concrete, day-by-day business of democracy, will put that fire there.

THE PROBLEM OF GERMANY

JOSEPH L. HROMÁDKA

Guest Professor, Princeton Theological Seminary;
formerly of the John Huss Faculty, Charles University, Czechoslovakia

I

THE IMMINENCE OF THE MILITARY DEFEAT OF GERMANY HAS accented the gravity of the question of what to do with her and how to reorganize the area between France and the Soviet Union. The literature dealing with this problem amounts to an enormous library. There is no end to conferences, forums, panels, and committee meetings which try, honestly and laboriously, to shed some light on the agonizing situation of Europe in general and of Germany and the German-occupied countries in particular. "The German problem" reveals, in an astounding way, the degree of the crisis and confusion in which modern humanity finds itself. We face today a much more complicated task than the leading statesmen of 1918 confronted. The disintegration of the pre-Munich international organization has surpassed anything the history of our civilization has witnessed since the early Middle Ages. In 1918 there was an alternative to the tottering Kaiser regime. A well-organized Social Democratic party in close co-operation with the Catholic political elements had offered a promise of a new Germany which might be, with relative ease, integrated into the postwar order. Today we know well-nigh nothing of what kind of political forces might take over the reorganization of the post-Nazi Germany. We dream of potential, hidden elements of the anti-Nazi Germans who have defied the nazification and preserved a little of the old German liberal, socialistic, or Christian tradition. However, we do not know much about their actual strength, let alone their ability to replace the Nazis and transform the national and political life. The question with whom in Germany we are going to co-operate is at present unanswerable.

The general state of affairs is complicated by the collapse of France. Only after June of 1940 did we realize what Europe would be like without a powerful, free, liberty-loving France; without her the liberal structure of the European order has lost its backbone. This has a tremendous bearing on the problem of Germany. We are at a loss as to the future of the French nation, and to her ability to become once again one of the chief cobuilders of the postwar political organization.

Not the least disturbing factor of the present international state of affairs is the lack of any—at least, as far as we know—agreed-upon plan in regard to the future of Germany. This lack cuts across all the main members of the United Nations. Public opinion in the Western democracies is obviously divided. This is nothing new. The era between the two wars may be characterized as an era of confusion and improvisation on the part of the leading European statesmen. After the American withdrawal from international co-operation the picture of European political life grew almost pitiful, and Germany understood how to make advantage both of the British-French rivalry and of the conservative fear and trembling before the potential and imaginary dangers coming from the Soviet Union.

The last but not the least weakness of our present situation is, as it were, a spiritual and moral weariness of the Western democracies. At the end of the first World War, the warring nations were invigorated by great hope and expectation of a new, free, democratic order of good will and co-operation. The buoyant spirit of nineteenth-century optimism had not yet died out, and it manifested itself in the faith that the new experiment of the League of Nations might overcome the barriers between victors and vanquished. All peoples and nations would be free and would enjoy the benefits of a lasting peace! However, this hope and optimistic expectation was Utopian, indulging in the unwarranted assumption that the peace treaty would work automatically. Moreover, it disintegrated into a political disillusionment or into complacent self-isolation of many European countries. The peace had not been organized, and the weary mind of the liberal and democratic society was unable, or even unwilling, to understand the very nature of international affairs, of the dynamic totalitarian movements, and of all the dangers inherent in the increasing political chaos.

We have not as yet adequately overcome the fatigue of our minds. Behind our amazing technical and military achievements loom fear and anxiety which mar our plans and make us suspicious lest we be double-crossed and deceived. Every day brings a new evidence of the psychological and moral uneasiness. Many people blame the leading statesmen for their failure to lay down a definite scheme for the peace. Yet this failure is but a reflection of the general atmosphere in the liberal and democratic countries. We are united in the resistance to the common enemies, in the determination to win the war, but are uncertain as to the principles and basis on which to reorganize the world and how to solve the essential issues of the international life. It is this general mental and moral atmosphere that makes the problem of Germany so difficult and agonizing. Being uncertain about ourselves, we are uncertain about the postwar organization of the world in general and of Germany in particular.

II

For many centuries the Germans had exerted a far-reaching influence on the peoples of Central and Eastern Europe: in music, literature, philosophy, education, religion. As long as they did not raise a claim of political domination, their leadership was gratefully accepted. Every nation of Central and Eastern Europe is ready to admit a certain debt to the intelligence, industry, organizational skill, science, and philosophy of the German people. In the middle of the nineteenth-century there existed, at least for a while, a great hope that the politically disunited Germans would establish a political unity on a liberal and democratic basis, and become a natural bridge between the European West and Central Europe. The potential co-ordination of European nations on a more or less liberal and progressive ground, however, was frustrated by the political course of Prussia, which had—under Bismarck's guidance—made a decision to create one *Reich* by military force, coercion, and discipline. The liberal bourgeois elements in Germany yielded to the military and political leadership of Prussia, of her king and nobility, and gradually accepted her program of aggression and domination. The romantic and idealistic German philosophy of the first decades of the nineteenth century permeated German schools and universities and German intellectual life, accentuating the aggressive nationalistic and militaristic tendencies of the united German *Reich*.

Since the defeat of Austria in 1866, and especially since the victory of 1870, the German *Reich* had increasingly exerted pressure on Austria-Hungary and made all effort to use her as a tool and instrument for expansive designs in the direction of the East and the Balkans (*Drang nach Osten*). The lack of vision and understanding on the part of the Austrian statesmen for the needs and aspirations of the non-German and non-Hungarian nationalities, and their gradual surrender to the German expansive efforts, was one of the chief reasons of the eventual breakdown and disintegration of Austria-Hungary. The growing national consciousness of the Central European nationalities, and their longing for self-determination, had defied the German pressure and associated itself with the Western democracies.

Yet, even after the defeat of Germany in 1918, the chance of German leadership did not vanish. The period immediately following the Munich Agreement in 1938 offered the last opportunity to win the Central European peoples for some kind of willing co-operation with the Germans. The political prestige of the Western democracies had fallen below zero. The victims of Munich were disillusioned and embittered. Their neighbors were bewildered and lost all hope in the West. The vacuum created by the French surrender and the British abdication at Munich could have been easily and naturally filled up by the Germans. We all knew that this last chance was destoryed by a ruthless, unscrupulous action of the Nazi regime, an action which will for centuries serve as a classic example of political blindness and stupidity. Had the Germans manifested one iota of patient wisdom on the one hand and of chivalrous magnanimity on the other, they would have become natural and unrivaled leaders of Central Europe and the Balkans; and their prestige would have, for generations, undermined the international leadership of all liberal democracies. The history of the present time would have adopted a totally different character. In all probability the Soviet Union would have been forced—under continuous threat and in total isolation—to become a junior partner and a satellite in the new Axis enterprise; or she might have been, sooner or later, crushed by the joint effort of the Axis powers. Now Germany has, for generations, forfeited any right of leadership. The German war lords, confused by the astounding Nazi successes of 1936-39 and drunk with the ideology of the *Beyond Good and Evil,* lost their heads, dragged Europe into an unparalleled catastrophe, and destroyed for a long future the honor, glory, and prestige of their country. The nations living east of Germany are terrified at the possibility that a lack of mutual trust and genuine co-operation between the Western democracies and the Soviet Union might create a new political vacuum which would enable the Germans to recover their military power, to renew their aggressive effort, and to crush mercilessly all small neighbors forever.

III

Simultaneously, however, we realize that without a loyal and constructive co-operation on the part of Germany no durable and creative peace is possible. After the war an irresistible cry for a peaceful settlement of the German problem will sweep through the countries of Anglo-Saxon tradition, and a momentous question will arise as to the disposition and preparedness on the part of the Germans to become voluntary fellow builders of a new Europe and a new world. Is there any reasonable hope of winning over, in a more or less predictable time, the German people for a European order based on the classical, universally valid, spiritual and moral, philosophical and political motifs of our civilization? Is there in Germany any alternative to Hitler's regime?

This is our dilemma. On the one hand, we are increasingly distrustful of the German people—for the past, for the present, and for the future. Let us listen to the Germans in exile, to their continuous controversies, and we shall see how they disagree among themselves. Many of them have little certainty and hope that there exists any significant group willing to accept the defeat and integrate themselves into a real collaboration for a new, politically free, and socially progressive, organization of Europe. If any of the German exiles professes a belief in the progressive leftist forces which might be capable of setting up a democratic order, another German contridicts him and points to a total lack of any evidence in this respect. The mentality and behavior of the German prisoners of war here, in the U. S. A., give us little hope that the Germans would genuinely co-operate with the victors.

On the other hand, however, we see that the postwar situation in Europe—and in the whole world—will be immensely difficult unless we win the people of Germany for a loyal and genuine co-operation.

In other words, we do know today better than we knew yesterday that no half measures will work when this terrible war is over. The Italian situation indicates that whoever has been stained and contaminated by close co-operation with fascism should be, for the benefit of the whole world, eliminated from any active participation in the new political order. The total war in which we are engaged has advanced beyond any wars and peace settlements in the past. The Italian regime must bear all the consequences of its political blunders, of its responsibility for the war, and of its defeat. The principles for which we are fighting contradict the very nature of the Axis regimes. What is at stake are the ultimate principles on which our moral and political order rests.

If it is true of Italy, how much more it applies to Germany! The Italian Fascism has never succeeded in merging its system with the Italian political character, whereas in Germany the situation seems to be different. We may, and should, avoid the equation of Germany and Nazism. We may, and should, see the dividing line between the classic German civilization and the National Socialist ideology and practice. Nevertheless, the Germany of the last eighty years has been the main agency of expansive, aggressive militarism. The German nation has become, on a large scale, the instrument of an unprecedented tyranny, brutality, and political reaction. Only a weak sentimentalism and relativistic indifference can justify Germany on the ground that Hitler has had many non-German predecessors in violence, unscrupulousness, and expansion, or that the German nation is not responsible for Hitler's crimes and atrocities. A clear, honest, realistic approach to the historical events in Germany and among the German-speaking people beyond the boundaries of the *Reich* reveals the agonizing fact that the majority of the Germans had followed Hitler of their free volition and made him capable of what he has done after he seized the power in 1933.

And yet, Germany must be reincorporated into the peace settlement; and the German people must—in some not-too-distant future—enjoy all the benefits of a lasting peace and prosperity. What are we to do in order to avoid both any

49

sentimental weakness and any measures that might make her future co-operation impossible?

IV

Now, what is the interrelation between the German people and Hitlerism? Is the Nazi ideology and practice a genuine expression of German history or an alien, destructive phenomenon imposed upon Germany by a group of tyrannical, brutal, abnormal gangsters, and adventurers? Is Germany the first country subjugated by the Nazis, and thus a fellow sufferer with other Nazi-occupied nations, as the Bishop of Chichester would like to have it? Or is Hitler just the right manifestation of the German mind on the way to world domination? Is Hitler, Germany? Is Germany, Hitler?

If we start from the international policy of the German *Reich*, we cannot overlook the continuity between the present Hitlerian drive and the pre-Nazi political mood of the German intelligentsia. William E. Dodd, American Ambassador to Germany 1934-38, was shocked by many evidences of the aggressive imperialism among his German personal friends who were anti-Nazi, very critical of Hitler, and still without any resentment toward his Eastern *Drang*. "Practically all Germans," he said, "want to control, if not annex, everything between their present eastern boundary and the Black Sea—not even an educated Republican German objects to the great risks in this direction. . . . The best of the Germans find it impossible to forgive the United States for participating in the World War. The Germans do not discuss this—but they feel that a great victory over all Europe was denied them."

No observer of German life and thought—even long before Hitler—could have failed to come to the same conclusion. By the end of the nineteenth century Edward von Hartmann, a philosopher of morbid pessimism, advocated a harsh policy against the Poles ("*Ausrotten!*"). Theodor Mommsen, one of the greatest German historians, encouraged the Austrian

Germans in their ruthless struggle against the Slavs. Wilhelm Herrmann, a gentle Protestant theologian of prewar Germany, was ready to justify, from his ethical point of view, the German *Drang nach Osten* on the basis of what Luther, Kant, and Goethe had achieved in the realm of faith, philosophy, and literature. Another German theologian, Friedrich Naumann, published in 1915 a book about Central Europe, *Mitteleuropa*, which has been in many ways a tentative blueprint for the forthcoming German aggressive actions. All these men and thinkers were certainly not rare and untypical spokesmen of the German mind.

Leopold Schwarzschild's book, *World in Trance*, 1942, interprets German history between the two wars as a gradual resurgence of the prewar ruling class. This class, embodied in the old Kaiser-army and later on in the *Wehrmacht*, had —in his judgment—never given up. It had been the driving force behind all the political changes after the war, even behind Hitler, intriguing and preparing for a new war. The German governments were, after Versailles, refractory, not because Germany had been compelled to sign the treaty, but because they were not forced to abide by the signature. Schwarzschild, and F. W. Foerster with very much the same emphasis, disputes the usual interpretation of the collapse of the Versailles system as a result of too harsh treatment of Germany. To the contrary, they say, the present catastrophe is due to the same latent aggressive tendencies of the German ruling class which were largely responsible for the first war and were carelessly left intact after the peace of 1919. Or, in other words, Hitler's international adventure is a direct continuation of the imperial Germany.

It is advisable to take this theory into a careful consideration. We are under temptation to identify any anti-Nazi sentiment in Germany with the opposition to Hitler's eastern and international policy. There exists a vigorous German nationalism which emotionally detests the Nazi movement but which, nonetheless, is in a full accord with its expansive militarism. There are many Christian philosophers and theologians in Germany who oppose Hitler on the ideological ground and who are, eventually, ready to face a persecution but who have never declined to affirm Hitler's conquests and international victories notwithstanding.

V

There is, however, another problem we have to deal with: How far is the Nazi ideology rooted in the spiritual and national tradition of Germany?

The Nazi thinkers have set up a theory that Hitlerism is a volcanic and final eruption of the genuine Teutonic soul through the veneer of the Greek (rational), Roman (legal), Jewish (moral), and Christian (sentimental) tradition which had covered and corroded the German national character. There exists a huge library of books and pamphlets that interpret the German history as a tragic conflict between the original, pagan, mystical, irrational elements of the Teutonic soul on the one hand and the alien, primarily Jewish and Christian, import on the other. The pure, creative, pagan soul of the Germanic race had resisted, and eventually under Hitler was able to prevail and to initiate a new era of a racially and spiritually genuine Teutonic creativity and domination. The Siegfried saga, Kaiser Frederick II (thirteenth century), the German mysticism of Meister Eckhart, Martin Luther, German pietism, Frederick the Great, Schleiermacher, Fichte, Romanticism, Nietzsche, Richard Wagner, Bismarck, Hitler, are the high marks of the all-powerful Germanic racial drive. Wilhelm Hauer, Herbert Grabert, W. Stapel, A. Deutelmoser, Alfred Rosenberg, and many others represent this philosophy of German history and contend that the Hitlerian movement marks the final victory of the Teutonic spirit over anything that had brought contamination and corruption into the German soul.

A caution is needed lest we accept the Nazi philosophy as an adequate interpretation of German history. However, there are other non-Nazi historians and philosophers who confirm—in a qualified way—some theses of the Nazi theory. Wilhelm Dilthey anticipated, half a century ago, in his philosophical sketches on German history, many aspects of the Nazi movement. He pointed to a thousand years of the German people's living in the forest. This fact shaped, in his judgment, the German character and mentality. The conduct of the Germans is not determined and limited by the setting up of rational objectives. There is something irrational in their actions, "The foolishness of unbridled passion." And if you examine Ernst Troeltsch's contributions to the understanding of German history, you may more deeply perceive why the German way of thinking has been responsible for the rise of Nazism. The concept of "individuality," the romantic emphasis upon individual uniqueness common to all religions and races, penetrated into the very heart of German thought and destroyed in it all universally valid principles and norms to which any man and any race ought to be subordinate, and thus cleared the road for both the specific value and the absolute autonomy of every race and for sheer power as the only conclusive court of appeal in the struggle between races.

Friedrich W. Foerster stresses primarily the Prussian background of Nazism. It is here that the Germanic irrational volcano has found its outlet. Prussia may be characterized as a sinister synthesis of irrational, spiritually and morally undisciplined chaos and of a rigid regimentation of barracks and officers' corps. Prussia absorbed, in Foerster's judgment, the national idea of the French Revolution and transformed it into a metaphysical and Teutonic fury. Bismarck's policy, rooted in the sinister tradition of the Prussian German Order of the Middle Ages and of their heirs, the Junkers, united the Germans by power and sword, and thus set up a pattern for the future and paved the road for Hitler.

Karl Barth, a Swiss, perhaps the most outstanding theologian of Europe, put it lately in a very similar way:

The German people suffer from a heritage of a paganism that is mystical and that is in consequence unrestrained, unwise, and illusory. And it suffers from the heritage of the greatest Christian of Germany, from Martin Luther's error on the relation between Law and Gospel, between the temporal and the spiritual order and power. This error has established, confirmed, and idealized the natural paganism of the German people, instead of limiting and restraining it. . . . Hitlerism is the present evil dream of the German pagan who first became Christianized in a Lutheran form.

Karl Barth's thesis points to the tremendous question as to what has been the weakness of German Protestantism and who has been most responsible for the Nazi movement. Who? Whereas Karl Barth seems to confirm F. W. Foerster's analysis of Nazism as a manifestation of the Prussian underground paganism, Hermann Rauschning, the author of *The Revolution of Nihilism* and *The Consecrative Revolution*, objects to this interpretation—all his books amount to a vigorous apology of the Prussian spirit. "Prussia," he says, "had much more of a nature of Puritanism, with a deep piety beneath its rough exterior, than one of militarism." Nazism is rather a modernized restoration of the great Spanish-German-Netherland empire of Charles V. The world of southern and southwestern Europe in the grip of Spanish fanaticism, Austrian and Bavarian romanticism, Jesuitism, Machiavellism, not the sober, practical Prussian north, may serve—says Rauschning—as a parallel of the Nazi *Reich*. Nazism is, furthermore, Marxism rampant. Hitler is much more indebted for his ideas of war and dynamism to socialist than to Prussian thinkers—to Proudhon, Sorel, Lenin. Nazism is the last stage of development in the process of secularization. It is the St. Vitus's dance of the nineteenth century.

T. G. Masaryk, a Czech philosopher and statesman, came, in his analysis of the modern mind—to a conclusion that it had been precisely in Germany that destructive Titanism, the mood of pessimism, irrationalism, and fatalistic despair

54

assumed a specific character and drove toward state absolutism and the warlike spirit:

The German superman, the Titan, is a nervous creature who seeks relief from chronic excitement in death (suicide) or in war. However true of all the nations this may be, it is especially true of the Germans. Their philosophers, artists and other active minds pushed subjectivism and individualism to absurd egomania, with all its moral consequences. In their spiritual isolation the German philosophers and men of learning, historians and politicians proclaimed German civilization and culture as the zenith of human development; and in the name of their arrogant claim to superiority, Prussian Pan-Germanism asserted its right to expansion and to the subjugation of others by sheer force. The Prussian State, its army and its fighting spirit became antidotes to morbid subjectivism.[1]

VI

There is little disagreement on the point of German responsibility for Hitler. Some thinker may interpret Nazism as an offshoot of Prussia, another as a reflection of Spanish fanaticism and southern-German romanticism; yet all of them see the organic interrelation between the Nazi movement and German history. The Germany of the last eighty years has been the main agency of political reaction and expansion.

But is Nazism identical with the German tradition? Are the Germans, by their very nature, by their innate character, Nazis? Here the answer is almost unanimously in the negative. T. G. Masaryk, who so severely criticized Prussianism and even in Goethe detested his "boundless egoism" as "a golden bridge to Prussian pan-Germanism," was an admirer of Beethoven, Bach, Herder, and Leibniz. "In Beethoven I see a German genius unspoiled by Prussia." He deplored the fact that "the splendid, noble and beauteous music of Germany had taken too light a hold on the hearts of [German] peoples." There exists another Germany.

[1] *The Making of a State*, George Allen & Unwin, Ltd., 1927.

The nazification of the German nation, and especially of the youth, has been profound; and nobody is in a position to fathom what has been left of the noble spiritual and literary tradition of great German thinkers. Nevertheless, there is hope that the forthcoming catastrophe of the German *Reich* will shake the mind of the people to its very depths, and create prerequisites for a better future.

How "the German problem" is to be solved nobody can say. We may agree on some points which seem to be essential and inevitable:

Germany must suffer a decisive military defeat. Any negotiated peace, without a total military collapse or surrender, would be disastrous.

The German war machine must be destroyed and the warlords—Hitler and his Party, the Elite Guard, the generals, the Junkers, the big men of industry and finance—liquidated.

The subjugated countries must be given back whatever the Nazi regime and the German Army have taken from them—territory; economic, artistic, educational, and technical equipment; and so forth.

Germany must be prevented from obtaining any economic supremacy in Europe and from the possibility of taking advantage of her economic power for rearmament.

All men responsible for this war, for cruelties and atrocities inflicted upon the victims of their lust for power and domination, must be punished. This is not a matter of vengeance and vindictiveness; it is rather a matter of justice without which any human society and civilization loses its backbone and foundation.

The occupation of Germany for a considerable time seems to be equally essential.

However, all these measures have just a negative meaning and cannot possibly construct a new basis for the German internal life and a loyal co-operation between the victors and the vanquished. How the positive reconstruction of Germany could be achieved I do not know. It is very difficult to be optimistic. Most of the political "realists" foresee and predict a dark future pregnant with new tragedies and catastrophes. They do not believe in either the possibility of a real change in the German soul or the political and moral wisdom of the victorious nations. They may be right. And yet, pessimism is no solution. A fatalistic skepticism is self-destructive. We must combine earnest, realistic understanding of the situation with the strenuous effort for a constructive program.

All will depend on whether or not the German mind will change and readjust itself to Europe. We know nothing about a political alternative to the Nazi regime. It may be totally absent, and any revolt against Hitler well-nigh impossible. The German Army and its generals were for some time regarded as a potential authority which might—against Hitler and the Party—take over the government, preserve the order, and offer its services to the people. An army revolt, however, is much more difficult at present than under the Kaiser. The army has not the monopoly of power. Hitler's bodyguard, the Gestapo, and the Elite Guard would in all probability back Hitler and the Nazi regime and foment a civil war of unprecedented dimensions. No wonder that the generals hesitate to give up Hitler. The German intelligentsia is politically immature. Germany lacked, for centuries, an adequate political education. Her thinkers paid little attention to the realm of political responsibility, civil rights, civil courage, and civil freedom. The amazing discipline and efficiency of civil servants, or the political indoctrination and regimentation under the Nazis, cannot be compared to the political dignity, maturity, and initiative of democratic citizens. It is primarily in Germany that the state has assumed an unrivaled position of absolute, supreme power, being regarded as the supreme criterion of all human aspirations. (Hegel!)

The process of readjustment and of the reintegration of Germany into the international community will be slow.

And yet, difficult as the problem is, there are some bright aspects of the situation.

I am not speaking of the dismemberment of Germany. There are some Germans who advocate it. Fritz Thyssen, a German industrialist, a onetime supporter of the Nazi movement, put it in a most unqualified way:

> The sadistic anti-Semitism of the Prussians, so foreign to our Rhineland population, the attempts to revive a barbaric paganism, have convinced me that the salvation of Germany, and of Europe, demands the restoration of the former barrier between these peoples.

Many men with a thorough knowledge of the German people contend that in the moment after the German war machine has been destroyed and the war lords have been liquidated Germany, in her present structure, will of necessity disintegrate, because the Army, the barracks, and the military aristocracy created the German *Reich* and have been its integrating and unifying force: any state stands and falls with the ideas, principles, and institutions which have been instrumental in creating it. I am personally inclined to agree with this opinion. No deliberate plan on the part of the victors to destroy the unity of the German people of 1870-1938 will produce permanent results. If, however, Germany disintegrates from within—and it is not absolutely impossible—then there may be a starting point for a reorganization and federalization of the German people on a more human, enlightened, free, and democratic basis, on a basis which would reflect more adequately the classic elements of the common European tradition.[2]

[2] Since this lecture was delivered, stunning events have taken place in Germany. The generals revolted and, on July 20, 1944, made an attempt to assassinate Hitler. They utterly failed, and the Nazis are now crushing—by executions and concentration camps—the very structure of the Germany of 1870. Hitler has become not only destroyer of the Greater (Nazi) Germany, and self-executioner, but also killer of the Germany as it was created and integrated by the Prussian army and the Junkers (Bismarck and Company). This is an event of enormous historical significance. The disintegra-

The collapse of the Nazi regime will produce in Germany such a profound political, moral, psychological, and spiritual shock that even the generation which has been reared and bred on the Nazi nourishment and under the absolute Nazi control *may* become approachable and more open to the ideals and motifs of humanity, liberty, and Christian mercy. These motifs are not wholly absent in the German history; they have been increasingly obscured by the emphasis on race, natural instinct, blood, power, domination, brutal force, and superman. The German history is, as we have already heard, a tragic conflict between the classical Christian civilization and the pagan Teutonic tradition. The Nazis have been convinced of the final victory of paganism over the German people. May not the very moment of their defeat mark the turning point, provided the victorious nations will have a constructive plan and co-operate among themselves in the spirit of mutual confidence?

On whom in Germany can we rely? It is difficult to say. The disillusioned youth *may* become the most zealous apostle of the new Germany. Some radical socialistic groups will in all probability be another rallying point; also genuine Catholics and some few Protestant believers who have proved sound, faithful in their convictions, and adamant in their burning determination to protect the freedom of the Church. The change and regeneration will be painful, and the re-education can be carried out only by the Germans themselves. We have no slight idea of who might reorganize the German people. And yet, we hope against hope; and our hope will not be in vain.

Hitler and Nazism are more than a purely German phenomenon. Nazism is the last stage of development in the general process of a de-Europeanization—a philosophical, moral, and spiritual disintegration. The German nation has

---

tion of Germany, and her partition, appear today more likely than they did some few months ago.

only the dubious merit to have become—because of some peculiar tendencies of German history—its carrier, representative, and instrument. However, the body of the whole modern society has been infected with the bacilli of cynicism, spiritual indifference, pessimism, and fatalism which are the incubators of tyranny and unfreedom. Only a tremendous spiritual struggle against the powers of evil, within and without, will be able not only to crush Hitler but to lay new, reliable foundations of a new world and of a new order.

THE TREATMENT OF A DEFEATED JAPAN [1]

T. A. BISSON

Member Research Staff, Institute of Pacific Relations

THE CLIMAX OF THE WAR IN EUROPE ADDS A NEW URGENCY to our planning for the peace that must be made with a defeated Japan. As the Cairo conference has demonstrated, this is no hypothetical question to be postponed for settlement *in toto* at some future peace conference. The terms of peace with Japan are already being laid down; as the war continues, they are certain to be further elaborated. There need be no quarrel with this procedure, which can be turned into a useful political adjunct of the military operations. Full correspondence and direct continuity between the political offensive and the final peace terms will contribute materially to the stability of the postwar settlement. As military success becomes assured, the outlines of a peace for the enemy people may be stated in more specific and more convincing terms. In the case of Europe, the political offensive is already passing over into the elaboration of a general program in which the German people can be expected to co-operate in the postwar world.

Events have not yet reached this stage in the Far East. Nor will victory in Europe automatically lead to the collapse of Japanese power, for Japan is too well entrenched behind its geographical ramparts on the Asiatic mainland and its oceanic and insular barriers in the Pacific. At the same time, the effects of Germany's defeat should not be discounted; they should rather be appraised at their right value and utilized

[1] Published as "The Price of Peace for Japan" in *Pacific Affairs*, March, 1944.

61

to the utmost. The end of the war in Europe will have a terrific impact upon Japan. It will erase all prospect of victory, even for the toughest core of Japan's military rulers. For the first time they will be forced to begin reckoning seriously with reactions on the home front. They will be concerned, above all, to prevent the realization of inevitable defeat from sinking deeply into the minds of the Japanese people. At this point the effective conduct of the war against Japan begins to merge with the problems of the peace.

In its initial stage, the peace settlement is in effect a political offensive conducted against the enemy nation with the object of weakening its will to resist. An adequate campaign of psychological warfare is double-pronged. It must, on the one hand, convince the masses of the enemy population that military defeat is inevitable, that the aims and objectives for which their leaders took them into the war cannot be achieved—are, in fact, irretrievably lost. On the other, it must offer specific alternatives for the period after defeat that will appeal to the same enemy populations as desirable—if possible, even more desirable than the strong emotional satisfactions deriving from empire, conquest, domination, and "master race" concepts. It is not enough to crush the enemy people's faith in their old leaders and to disillusion them in the virtue of the old program. Pledged support for a new leadership and a new program is required if hope and activity are to replace despair and apathy in the defeated peoples. Confidence must be created in the belief that something positive and constructive can be built on the ruins of defeat. On this dynamic factor new forces can rise in the enemy countries to challenge the old, making themselves felt at first in the final episodes of the war and then in the the shaping of a better postwar society.

This pattern of a double-pronged psychological offensive, organically linking the conduct of the war to the making of the peace, has already emerged clearly in Europe. In his broadcast following the Teheran conference, President

Roosevelt expressed the general principles underlying the political attack on Germany in most careful and exact terminology. The conferees at Teheran, said the President,

were united in determination that Germany must be stripped of her military might and be given no opportunity within the foreseeable future to regain that might.

The United Nations have no intention to enslave the German people. We wish them to have a normal chance to develop, in peace, as useful and respectable members of the European family. But we most certainly emphasize that word "respectable"—for we intend to rid them once and for all of Nazism and Prussian militarism and the fantastic and disastrous notion that they constitute the "master race."

Against the background of the final military assault on the European fortress, three simple principles are laid before the German people: (1) Germany's military power will be crushed and not permitted to revive; (2) the old leadership must go; and (3) on these bases, the German people will again be accepted as normal members of the European community. The uncompromising nature of this program is perhaps its most striking feature. Even with respect to the second principle, there is no call to the Germans to throw out their old leaders. The words used—"we intend to rid them"—place the responsibility on the United Nations for this drastic action. They are an implied threat to those Germans who support the old leaders, and an implied promise to those Germans who would like to see them overthrown. Co-operation of the German people in this overthrow would obviously be welcomed, but it is neither urged nor suggested.

In the same broadcast President Roosevelt also made reference to two basic elements which enter into the making of peace with Japan. First there must be "the restoration of stolen property to its rightful owners"—a restatement of the Cairo pledge that Japan will be stripped of all territories gained by aggression since 1895; and, secondly, the peace will ensure "the permanent elimination of the Empire of

Japan as a potential force of aggression." It is noteworthy that these two pronouncements, taken together, do not go beyond the first principle as stated for Germany. They constitute a blunt affirmation of the intention of the United Nations to fight the war against Japan to a finish, somewhat analogous in this respect to the "unconditional surrender" demand voiced at Casablanca. It might have been assumed that further statements on Japan, covering the scope of the last two principles set forth for Germany, would have to wait upon victory in Europe and the mounting of the final assault against Japan. At this point, however, Generalissimo Chiang Kai-shek, in a New Year's message to the Chinese Army and people, went far to close the gap. Revealing a hitherto unreported passage at the Cairo conference, he made the following statements:

In intimate talks I had with President Roosevelt and Prime Minister Churchill at Cairo we considered steps for mutual co-operation and agreed upon certain plans for prosecution of the war.

We also agreed upon the question of the disposal of the enemy after the war. One important problem in this connection concerns Japan's form of government. When President Roosevelt asked my views I frankly replied: "It is my opinion that all Japanese militarists must be wiped out and the Japanese political system must be purged of every vestige of aggressive elements. As to what form of government Japan should adopt, that question can better be left to the awakened and repentant Japanese people to decide for themselves."

I also said, "If the Japanese people should rise in revolution to punish their war mongers and overthrow their militarists' government we should respect their spontaneous will and allow them to choose their own form of government." Mr. Roosevelt fully approved of my idea.[2]

Assuming that these statements reflect a common approach to the peace settlements in Europe and the Far East, it is al-

[2] *New York Times*, January 3, 1944.

ready possible to sketch the type of peace to be made with Japan. A few of the outlines are even now sharp and clear; others must be drawn on the basis of given suggestions in the light of objectives which seeem desirable.

The peace with Japan will be a harsh one in many of its aspects, notably those affecting territories, disarmament, and possible reparations. When the costs and sacrifices of defeating Japan's ruthless aggression are placed in the reckoning, nothing less should be expected or desired. These terms of the peace will, in some cases, be setting right old wrongs that have endured for a generation or longer. They are also required to limit Japan's power to engage in a second adventure in aggression.

Obviously, these terms presuppose the existence and continued maintenance of unity between members of the United Nations and the emergence of a strong and effective international organization. Continued agreement and firm cooperation, at least among the United States, Great Britain, the U.S.S.R., and China, are indispensable in order to enforce the terms of peace against Japan initially and then to see that they are upheld. Given this degree of unity, the harsher aspects of the peace can be mitigated somewhat by measures which will indicate clearly to the Japanese people that the settlement is dictated not by a policy of revenge, nor with an intention to enslave. The line is not so difficult to draw as might appear. A vengeful peace can be defined as one aimed at keeping Japan in a state of lasting subjection, political or economic. Any such policy would be self-defeating. Sir George Sansom has rightly declared that the existence of "a nation of over seventy million desperate and frustrated people would ruin any plan designed to bring prosperity and peace to Asia." [3] The principle enunciated by President Roosevelt for the German people must also be taken as applying to the Japanese people—they will be given "a normal

[3] *Postwar Relations with Japan*, Mont Tremblant Conference Documents, Secretariat Paper No. 2, p. 4.

chance to develop, in peace, as useful and respectable members" of the world community.

What is stated here really amounts to a process of postwar development. It looks toward the emergence of a healthy Japan which can in time re-enter the society of nations as a member in full standing. The process makes serious demands on the United Nations as well as on Japan. They must assist her to develop along peaceful lines on both the political and economic levels; they must assume direct responsibility for the type of political and social structure established in Japan after her defeat. United Nations' guidance will be required, in greater or lesser degree, to make it certain that the old autocratic system is not re-established, but that a new system is inaugurated in which the democratic aspirations of the Japanese people find real expression. Full opportunity must also be given Japan to raise the living standard of her people by the processes of normal international trade. The new world organization must have not only the strength to maintain collective security but also the economic statesmanship to eliminate trade barriers and develop the colonial areas of the world by measures for improving the social and economic welfare of the inhabitants, on a basis of nondiscriminatory international co-operation. This process will provide the most dependable safeguard against renewed Japanese (or German) aggression. The enemy nations must be restored to health and then must be fitted into a constructive system of international collaboration.

It thus becomes evident that the harsher aspects of the peace settlement constitute merely the preliminary and not the most important stage. They represent nonetheless an indispensable foundation which must be carefully laid. It is essential, above all, that these punitive terms not be applied in such fashion as to jeopardize the constructive ends in view. Fortunately, the largest measure of agreement will probably be found among the United Nations on this phase of the settlement.

THE TREATMENT OF A DEFEATED JAPAN

It may be taken for granted that the decision of the Cairo conference to strip Japan of her territorial acquisitions since 1895 will be enforced. In all territories there enumerated, Japan is now ruling peoples other than her own; this privilege will certainly be taken from her. In territory and population, what does this mean for Japan? Before the Treaty of Shimonoseki in 1895, Japan was a nation of some forty million people living mainly on the 148,000 square miles of its home islands. Today Japan controls, in round numbers, an area of three million square miles inhabited by five hundred million people. After the peace she will have about seventy-five million Japanese, again living mainly on the restricted area of her home islands.

Along with this drastic change will go a series of strict disarmament provisions. The greater part of Japan's navy will conceivably be sunk during the later phases of the war; what remains will have to be surrendered. Munitions of war, including military aircraft, will also have been destroyed or, if not, will have to be turned over to the United Nations. Munitions plants will either be destroyed or forced to undergo conversion to production of peacetime goods. For a period of years, which will probably not be definitely fixed, Japan will be prohibited from maintaining a naval or military force of any kind. A civilian police force will alone be permitted.

Thus far it may be assumed that little disagreement would exist. More extreme proposals call for the total abolition of Japanese industry and the return of that country to an agrarian subsistence economy. Since proposals of this kind would condemn possibly one-quarter of Japan's present seventy-five million people to death by starvation, it would seem the part of wisdom to discount and reject them. Extermination is not a rational solution to the problem. Persons advocating such methods are evading the real task which faces the United Nations—the bringing into existence of a decent Japan which can co-operate with other nations in establishing an enlightened world community.

In one other aspect of Japanese disarmament, however, it might be advisable to impose even stricter conditions than are generally suggested. This affects the treatment of the Japanese officer class, military and naval, which has largely supplied the Hitlers and the Himmlers of Japan, the spearheads of Japan's totalitarianism. The principle of the punishment of German and Italian leaders guilty of committing criminal acts, clearly stated in the Moscow agreements, should be applied also to the Japanese. In the case of Japan a further step should be adopted. To allow the officer class in general to enjoy full freedom and immunity would be exceedingly prejudicial to the emergence of a democratic Japan in the postwar era. Officers of the rank of lieutenant colonel and naval captain upwards might have to be interned or exiled for a number of years after the war. If a method of training them in more democratic ways can be applied during this period, so much the better. In any case, the free circulation of this group of officers inside Japan during the immediate postwar years would seriously jeopardize all that we should hope to see develop there.

On reparations, there is likely to be considerable difference of opinion. It is only natural that the Chinese people, conscious of the devastation wrought in their country since 1937, should insist that full reparation be made for the injury suffered. Part of this reparation, at least, may be obtained in the recovered territories. The Chinese will inherit important and sizeable industrial installations in Manchuria and Formosa, unless extensive damage is caused later on by bombing raids or a "scorched earth" policy. Particularly in Manchuria, with its coal and iron mines, blast furnaces, and rolling mills (producing today more than a million tons of steel annually), China will obtain an increment of heavy industry of significant proportions. It might be well to transfer to China on reparation account all Japanese vested interests in Manchuria and Formosa, without regard to the present legal character of the titles; the same principle could also be applied, with a considerable degree of justice in Korea.[4] This type of action would be doubly advantageous. At one stroke it would settle the intractable issues clustering around Japanese "rights and interests" in these territories, mostly gained by force and chicanery, which helped to precipitate the Manchurian invasion in September, 1931. Joined to restoration of Chinese sovereignty, it would give China full mastery in the regained territories. It would have the further advantage of telescoping reparations into a single, well-defined act, thus avoiding the handicap to restoration of normal economic and psychological conditions which long-drawn-out reparations payments bring in their train.

Strong reasons can be mustered against the advisability of exacting further reparations of any considerable scope from Japan. Thrown back on the narrow limits of its home islands, Japan will be faced at best with an exceedingly onerous task of self-support. Extreme proposals calling for the transfer of the equipment of Japan's home industry to China or other Far Eastern countries have a dubious validity. Aside from their uneconomic character, such proposals are merely another way of insisting that Japan return to its agrarian economy of a century ago, previously noted as an irrational extermination policy. If the proposals seek merely the transfer of presently existing equipment, leaving Japan free to replace it, then one can be sure that Japan will replace it with new and better machinery within five or ten years. Actually, there is no valid reason for placing artificial barriers in the path of Japan's economic progress. With the security issue settled, it may be assumed that Japan's economic advance will be to the advantage and not the detriment of all other Far Eastern countries. Disarmament and security provisions

[4] This principle might be extended to other less important spheres of Japanese investment in the Far East and in Western countries. Japanese vested interests in all these areas could be impounded as reparations, to be allocated to China or other members of the United Nations. It has also been suggested that Japanese technicians might be required to facilitate the transfer to Chinese management of such enterprises as exist in Manchuria.

should be kept in their own proper sphere, where the terms already envisaged will leave Japan hopelessly weak for a long period of years. It is not advisable that reparations be used as an indirect means of disarmament by keeping a country weak through an enforced economic backwardness. This, too, is a method that dodges the central task of restoring the enemy country to political and social health and enabling it to play a constructive role in an expanding world economy.

Consideration of the punitive aspects of the peace settlement continually emphasizes the fact that these terms are not the ends in view. They are means to a quite different end. Disarmament that must be forever enforced by an outside authority has failed in its true objective—that is, to allow for the lapse of a sufficient period within which the ex-enemy nation will reorient its economy and its politics toward peace. If this reorientation is not achieved, then it may be questioned whether any measures of disarmament can be so strictly enforced for so long a period of time as to prevent some ultimate day of revival and renewal of aggression by the subjected nation. With the old forces in control of the country, the desire for revenge and the old type of conquest and aggrandizement will remain and will eventually find expression again, no matter what obstacles are reared against them.

The problem of establishing peace thus runs much deeper than the mere handling of disarmament issues. Extension of disarmament into the factory, a necessity under modern conditions, still treats the symptoms, not the disease itself. The key issue in the degree of success attending the United Nations' dealings with a defeated Japan is not how well the country is disarmed but how greatly its outlook and motivations are changed. In the last analysis, what is required is a thorough recasting of Japan's political and social leadership. Addressing himself to Germany, President Roosevelt declared in the statement already quoted: "We intend to rid them once and for all of Nazism and Prussian militarism and the fantastic and disastrous notion that they constitute the 'master race.'" In much the same terms, Generalissimo Chiang Kai-shek stated that "all Japanese militarists must be wiped out and the Japanese political system must be purged of every vestige of aggressive elements."

These declarations sweep away objections which are often heard when this question is raised. Who are we to meddle with Japan's form of government? Can we expect to impose democracy on Japan? Will the reaction not be worse than the cure? One answer, of course, is that we could not shuffle off the responsibility actually resting upon us for some decision in this field even if we wanted to. If the United Nations waive their responsibility and do nothing, we may be sure that the militarists sheltering behind their god-emperor will be back again in short order.

Another answer is that the Japanese people may be found capable of doing a good part of the job themselves. In that case, it would not be necessary to impose anything. It would merely be necessary to see that the Japanese militarists received no help in suppressing the expression of the people's wrath, in line with the statement made by Generalissimo Chiang Kai-shek. Such popular dissatisfaction with the old militarist regime will be uncovered in Japan after defeat has come, if it does not appear earlier. United Nations' administrators will find many persons well-disposed toward them, just as they find such persons in Italy; some of these will be political prisoners when the liberating forces land on the Japanese islands. It should not be forgotten that, even with the cards stacked against them, the Japanese people twice made use of their franchise to express their overwhelming opposition to the fascist encroachments at home and militarist aggression abroad—once on February 20, 1936, and again on April 30, 1937. The political parties, made the vehicle of these protest votes and controlled largely by the business monopolies which supported the militarists' aggressive program, could not but betray the people's hopes. Prince Konoye's war cabinet, supposedly formed on the basis of the election results of April 30, 1937, demonstrated the totally nonresponsible and nondemocratic character of the old regime by carrying the Japanese people into war with China three months later. But the people had, in fact, expressed themselves as against the war and the whole policy which it represented and carried forward. After the war they may find more effective means of demonstrating their real beliefs.

Very likely, however, some outside assistance may prove to be necessary. Can it be said, then, that the United Nations will lack the power to change the course of the political current in Japan and set it in the right direction? Consider Japan's position at the end of the war. Her colonial territories will be gone. The home islands will be devastated. Domestic production will be low, with consumers' goods virtually unobtainable. Few merchant ships will be left, and foreign trade will be nonexistent. The Japanese people will be hungry and exhausted. One of the first tasks will be to extend help; otherwise, no inconsiderable part of the population might face death from starvation. These factors together hardly suggest that United Nations' administrators in Japan will lack the authority requisite to enforce their will. Added to everything else will be the powers handed over by an unconditional military surrender amounting, for the period of military occupation at least, to the virtual transfer of Japanese sovereignty.[5]

It will be unnecessary to utilize this power in a way that will outrage the sentiments of the Japanese people and so create a festering desire for revenge. It will merely be necessary to use it in a way that will give full expression to the actual desires of Japan's hungry and oppressed masses. Japan is no "special case" in this respect, any more than in others.

[5] For discussion of these factors see A. J. Grajdanzev, "Future of a Defeated Japan," in *The Far East Draws Near*, Forum 3, pp. 1-5, of the Programs of the General Federations of Women's Clubs, Washington, D. C.

72

From among the Japanese will come the leaders who will be able to usher in the new democratic regime, if the administrators for the United Nations know what they are about and welcome and work with this new leadership and eschew the old. It will be the responsibility of such administrators to seek out the honest forces of opposition to the old regime and give them the help essential to its abolition. Barring a major social revolutionary upheaval, which would be a most useful instrument in cracking the encrusted tyranny of old Japan, the new Japan cannot be expected to emerge overnight. It will be a slow growth, requiring our most discerning guidance and careful nurture.

In this task it will be necessary to have a clear understanding of the old Japan which we are seeking to transform. Who are the forces that have ruled Japan, making it the predatory, aggressive power that it is today? As in Germany, they consist mainly of the large landlords, the big industrialists, and the Army, with its ruthless fanaticism, its ideology of the master race, and its spirit of aggressive conquest.

First of all come the landlords, corresponding in many ways to the Junker class in Germany. In 1938 there were 3,547 (0.7 per cent of the total number of landowners) of these landlords, each owning fifty *cho* (122.5 acres) or more of land.[6] The relatively small acreage in these figures is deceptive. Many of these large holders own considerably more than fifty *cho*; and, taken together, the 3,547 big landowners hold a considerable slice of the best arable land in Japan. Land is scarce; competition for the best plots is exceedingly fierce. So the price of farm land is very high—much higher, relatively, than in Western countries. Assume that the smallest big landowner, with fifty *cho*, holds the best type of land—the fertile paddy fields, or irrigated rice land. His fifty *cho* will be valued at about four hundred thousand yen, no small sum by the Japa-

[6] Shiroshi Nasu, *Aspects of Japanese Agriculture*, International Secretariat, Institute of Pacific Relations, 1941, p. 10.

nese standards. This smallest of Japan's big landowners is a large investor and he will require big profits, especially in a country where earnings of 15 to 20 per cent on industrial investments have been general. He is in many cases an absentee landlord, not even participating in the management of his estate.

It is also necessary to look at the other end of the scale in the Japanese countryside. Here we find three different groups: owners, tenants, and the part owners, owning some land outright and renting other plots in addition. In 1936 there was an aggregate total of 5,597,465 farm households in Japan. Of these, 1,731,139 were owners; 1,517,701 were tenants; and 2,348,625 were part owners. More than three million of the owners and part owners held less than one *cho* of land apiece, or somewhat less than 2.5 acres. More than two million owned less than half a *cho* apiece, or less than 1.25 acres. The tenant farmers were, in general, considerably worse off than the small owners. In 1938 tenant farmers worked 46.5 per cent, or nearly half, of all the land cultivated in Japan.[7] These data indicate the economic conditions which prevail in the Japanese countryside. At one end of the scale is a tiny minority of 3,547 wealthy and parasitic landlords; at the other, five and a half million tenant farmers and poverty-stricken small holders. It must be added that share-cropping rents of 50 to 60 per cent of the crop are common, that usurious interest rates tend to aggravate the burden of debt on the farmers, and that the taxation system has weighted proportionately more heavily on rural than on urban areas. When famine strikes Japan, it is the poverty-stricken rural areas that are hardest hit.[8] Little wonder that outbreaks of tenant-landlord disputes have worried the Japanese over-

[7] This figure includes the dry uplands as well as the irrigated rice fields.

[8] At present, war conditions tend to redress the balance, while in recent years the large rural-urban migration into war industries, by increasing the poor farmers' bargaining power, has also tended to better his conditions at least temporarily.

lords, even though these have been sporadic and localized since the "rice riots" of 1918. While the makings of a drastic peasant uprising exist in Japan, there is another side to the medal. The farmers have been the favored army conscripts, as the least affected by new-fangled ideas, the most fanatical adherents of the god-emperor, and thus the most robotlike cannon fodder. And so the militarists insist that the 40 per cent of Japan's population which now consists of farmers must not be allowed to decrease.

The second group in this trinity is the big industrialists, the *Zaibatsu* of Japan. These vast monopolistic family enterprises, the Mitsuis, Mitsubishis, and a half-dozen other combines, dominate the financial, industrial, and commercial life of Japan. The concentration of capital in this handful of Japanese banking and business monopolies is more extreme than in any other country. Recent figures on the growth of this concentration are not available; but at the beginning of the 'thirties, when Japan launched its latest movement of territorial expansion, the figures were already startling. The Big Three (Mitsui, Mitsubishi, and Sumitomo) held nearly 25 per cent of the banking capital of the whole country, while the Big Eight (adding Yasuda, Shibusawa, Kawasaki, Yamaguchi, and Konoike to the other three) held well over 50 per cent. The Big Five (Mitsui, Mitsubishi, Shibusawa, Yasuda, and Sumitomo) held nearly 40 per cent of total bank deposits, nearly 30 per cent of total loans, and nearly 45 per cent of the total security investments of the whole country. These figures reflect a situation prevailing some fifteen years ago. Since then the process of concentration, both in finance and industry, has moved forward swiftly. The Industrial Control Associations, set up at the outset of the Pacific War in 1942, were headed by the leaders of the former private cartels and were given direct official backing in the task of integrating smaller industrial units with the monopoly enterprises.

This is the picture shown at the top of Japan's business

75

and financial world. At the bottom of the ladder are the millions of overworked and miserably paid mine and factory operatives. The depressed wages of Japan's industrial workers are in large part maintained by virtue of the ever-present reservoir of new workers in the even more poverty-stricken countryside. This condition of Japan's competitive prowess was bluntly stated by Professor Nasu:

> Existence of up-to-date factories with high technical efficiency side by side with millions of small farms amply supplying these factories with skillful but low-wage man-power constitutes the backbone of the national economy of Japan. This relationship is made possible by the fact that the birth rate of the rural population is higher than that of the urban population.[9]

Here we have another reason for the deliberate attempt, this time on the part of the industrialists, to keep the farm population from dropping below the 40 per cent level. Professor Nasu's remarks also reveal one of the basic incentives to the intensity of Japan's drive for foreign markets. The home market, restricted by the low incomes of its workers and farmers, cannot begin to absorb the flood of goods produced by Japan's "up-to-date factories with high technical efficiency." But the "low-wage man-power" propels these goods into foreign markets with great competitive force. In these facts we see the interests of the big landlords and the industrial monopolists linked with the militarists in a drive for trade expansion which passes inexorably into territorial conquest.

The position and role of the militarists remain to be considered. In many respects they perform the key function in directing the aggressive side of Japanese imperialist expansion. It is sometimes asserted that Japan differs from Germany in that it has no totalitarian party. Until the suppression of the old-line political parties and the founding of the Imperial Rule Assistance Association in 1940, this assertion was super-

[9] Nasu, *Aspects of Japanese Agriculture*, p. 8.

ficially true, but only superficially. The Japanese militarists, without any formal organization, were the Nazi party of Japan for many years prior to 1940. They had their own means of appeal to the masses, through a host of chauvinist societies, and through inflammatory speeches and pamphlets circulating in hundreds of· thousands of copies. They utilized the Nazi methods of direct action, including assassination and overt uprisings. They held a decisive initiative in foreign policy through their assumed power of launching military operations in a foreign country on their own authority, irrespective of the policy of the cabinet that happened to be in office at the time.

These formidable powers enabled the militarists to do virtually everything that the Nazis were able to do in Germany.[10] And, unlike the Nazis, they controlled in and of themselves all the resources of the armed services of the state. There was no question of party agreement or disagreement with the Army; they *were* the Army, particularly since the late 'thirties when the extremist elements pushed aside the more moderate army leaders.

The militarists came to wield this tremendous power mainly because the constitution granted by the emperor in 1889 accorded the army and navy leaders direct access to the emperor and allowed them to exercise a political authority not possessed by the armed services of any other modern state. These powers enabled the Japanese militarists to arrogate the right of being the authorized interpreters of the emperor's will and of the mission of the "divinely-empowered" Japanese race. On this basis they developed an ideology thoroughly akin in spirit and purpose to the ideology of Hitlerism. Throughout the 'thirties they conducted an unrelenting campaign against all liberal attempts to define the emperor's posi-

[10] Their subordination of monopolist industrial enterprises to state control was achieved much later than in Germany and never so completely. See the writer's article, "Problems of War Production Control in Japan," *Pacific Affairs*, September 1943, p. 301.

tion in any way which would permit the evolution of a constitutional monarchy in Japan. Professor Minobe's textbooks, defining the emperor as an "organ of the state" rather than the "state itself," previously accepted as authoritative in all the universities from the Tokyo Imperial University down, were banned from the schools; and Minobe himself was compelled to resign from the House of Peers. This fact should give pause to those persons who advocate maintenance of the emperor as a "stabilizing force" in the Japanese political structure or who believe in the feasibility of establishing a liberal constitutional monarchy in Japan.

Still another aspect of the militarists' close ties with the emperor deserves careful attention. The army leaders have assiduously fostered the divine pretensions of the emperor as a tool of domestic and foreign policy. On the home front, this medieval ideology is utilized to cement morale, lead the masses to accept their subordinate status, and encourage them to endure the sacrifices and burdens of war. On the battlefield, it is used to instill a morale of fanaticism in the Japanese troops. Still more, it has enabled the ruling trinity to implant the "master race" theory in the consciousness of the Japanese people, leading them to believe that they are divinely ordained to rule the world. The first sentence of the Japanese Field Service Code, as revised in January 1941, reads as follows: "The battlefield is where the Imperial Army, acting under the Imperial command, displays its true character, conquering wherever it attacks, winning wherever it engages in combat, *in order to spread Kodo far and wide so that the enemy may look in awe to the august virtues of His Majesty.*" *Kodo* is the term usually translated as "Imperial Way," twisted by Japanese ideologists from the old Confucian interpretation of benevolent rule by a sage-king into the basis

[11] Similar use is made of *Hakko Ichi-u,* deriving from a Chinese Taoist term (*Pa Hung Yi Yü*) with a peaceful connotation figuratively rendered as "The Whole World Under One Roof," which has been widely applied by Japanese leaders as a synonym for bringing all nations under the sway of the emperor.

for a mission of world conquest.[11] It is noteworthy, moreover, that the Japanese have not been content to restrict
worship of the emperor to their own nationals. They have
also forced it on their subject nations, including those recently made "independent." Formosan and Korean subjects have
long been compelled to offer religious submission to the Japanese emperor. In Manchuria, and more recently in the Philippines and other vassal states in Southeast Asia, obeisance to
the emperor on special anniversaries in the Japanese religious
calendar has been forced upon Japan's new subjects. As in
the Roman parallel, this technique does not involve the suppression of other religions. All religious groups are maintained. They are sedulously courted in order to win their
support for the newly established regime; or else they are
played one against the other to weaken existing opposition
to Japanese domination.

In this field, it is generally agreed, lies one of the crucial
postwar decisions which the United Nations must make. If
the relationship of the Japanese militarists to the emperor is
maintained after the war, our victory will be hollow and our
sacrifices in vain. Sooner or later the forces of old Japan will
revive and again plunge the nation into a war to spread *Kodo*
over the world. It is essential that the whole imperial myth
be discredited in the minds of the Japanese people and the
possibility of its revival be forever removed. If the Japanese
people turn against the emperor and dethrone him, the act
should be applauded and supported. If they do not, the act
must be done for them as soon as their acquiescence can be
reasonably taken for granted.[12]

It will be argued that such a policy is not one that the
United Nations can undertake, since this is a most delicate

[12] The claim that the ruling emperor is a good and harmless man is be-
side the point. It is the institution which carries the danger. The same may
be said for the recent alleged "proof" in State Department documents that
Hirohito ordered the militarists to refrain from precipitating war with the
United States. See Wilfred Fleischer's dispatch, *New York Herald Tribune*,
December 12, 1942.

issue and the roots of emperor-worship are too deeply embedded in the consciousness of the Japanese. The answer to this objection is that no one expects to accomplish the result in a day or a month, or by fiat of an AMG. Only a deepseated revolution could effect the result overnight. It is vital, however, that conditions be established immediately after defeat which will divorce the emperor from the militarists and permit the free growth of rational ideas among the Japanese people. State Shinto, which embraces a compulsorily enforced belief in the emperor's "divine mission" to rule the world, should be banned as a manifestation of aggressive policy which the United Nations will not tolerate. It has already been made clear that the dissemination of Nazi ideology among the German people is not to be permitted after the defeat of Germany. Why, then, should such permission be granted to Japan's rulers?

Under arrangements which make forcible regimentation of belief in the state cult impossible, the discrediting of the god-emperor mythos in the minds of the Japanese people may not prove so difficult as many seem to imagine. Not a few Japanese have had reservations as to the orthodox Sun Goddess mythology.[13] Crushing defeat, in a war brought on by the emperor's chosen militarist ministers, will in itself constitute an educative influence of considerable value.[14] It should be borne in mind that much of the paraphernalia of the state cult is a relatively modern innovation, deliberately

[13] See D. C. Holton, *Modern Japan and Shinto Nationalism* (University of Chicago Press, 1943) pp. 52-54, 87. Careful study of this book is essential for all who may be called upon to make policy decisions in relation to Japan.

[14] Since it is the imperial institution that must be abolished, it is dubious strategy to try to dissociate the emperor from the militarists. This, in fact, would be the logical move for the militarists themselves to make under conditions of defeat, since it would enable them to lie low for a time while salvaging the institution for further use at some later period. Efforts to "dissociate" the emperor from his "evil" advisers, by tending to sanction the institution as such, will thus play into the hands of the very forces which we are trying to uproot.

brought into being by the early Meiji leaders. The custom of bowing to the emperor's portrait, for example, was not introduced until 1891. Moreover, the conditions of the modern world are not favorable to the maintenance of concepts such as those associated with the god-emperor cult in Japan. In the world of modern industrialism and science such myths tend to wither and die. These factors were obviously operating to good effect in Japan itself, as witnessed by the immense efforts made by the militarists to combat "dangerous thoughts" and reindoctrinate the nation in the tenets of the god-emperor cult throughout the decade of the 'thirties. Their struggle against Minobe has already been noted. The campaign really began much earlier when General Sadao Araki held the post of Inspector-General of Military Education at the close of the 'twenties and the opening of the 'thirties. Utilizing the advantages of this post, he thoroughly revised the educational program applied to the army conscripts, seeking to imbue them with his own fanatic adherence to *Kodo* and the nation's divine mission of conquest under the emperor. In the late 'thirties General Araki assumed the post of minister of education, from which vantage point he carried through the same "reform" of the school system's indoctrination courses that had been originally applied in the barracks. It is thus clear that the militarists recognize not only the value of this ideology but the obstacles to its full acceptance which exist in Japan today. Is this field to be resigned to the forces representing old Japan; or is every effort to be made, discreetly but nonetheless firmly, to guide the intellectual current in a direction that will help to bring into being the new Japan which is required in the interests of a peaceful world community?

This brief survey of the old Japan has reviewed some of the key forces which have operated to create the spirit of conquest that has plunged Asia into war. It is not necessary, after victory, that there be carried to Japan a complete blueprint of reform which shall then be forced *in toto* upon the

Japanese people. It *is* necessary that United Nations' administrators be thoroughly familiar with the old forces that have been operating there and that they should set a course that will prevent these old forces from reasserting control, on the one hand, and will encourage those new forces that will be able to bring into being a different Japan. The emphasis placed on the destruction of the emperor cult in this discussion indicates how essential it is for the new leadership to divorce itself from the myths of a past era which must of necessity operate perniciously in the modern world. New leaders must also be sought who will recognize that the relationship between the poverty-stricken farmers and low-wage industrial workers is a vicious phenomenon directly allied to the ability of the militarists to engross the powers of the state and, in alliance with the landlords and the great *Zaibatsu* magnates, to embark on a mission of world conquest. Agrarian reform, involving land redistribution and changes in the systems of land tenure and rural credit, is a prerequisite to the establishment of social and economic health in Japan. Improved living conditions for the farmers will force higher wage standards for the industrial workers by removing that inexhaustible reservoir of cheap labor on which the *Zaibatsu* have waxed fat. The resultant increase in purchasing power by the mass of the population will expand Japan's home market and thus reduce the pressure to export; by the same token, the higher cost of labor will diminish the keen edge of Japanese competition which Western merchants have experienced to their distress. An economic margin for these domestic reforms will be provided by the abolition of armament expenditures which have hitherto absorbed such a large proportion of Japan's national income.

The outside world will have to undergird this development by providing Japan with the fullest access to raw materials and markets. Foreign trade will be Japan's "lifeline" after the war in a sense quantitatively so enhanced as almost to make a qualitative difference. Large amounts of raw materials formerly within Japan's "domestic" sphere, notably in Manchuria, Korea, and Formosa, will henceforth be in foreign countries. Much of these will be absorbed locally, and so entirely removed from Japan's economic orbit. Similarly, the former Japanese-controlled markets in these territories will henceforth be foreign markets. Purchases may be made elsewhere, or tariffs may be instituted to protect developing industries. For a considerable period after the war, Japan may be expected to retain its chief competitive advantage—the production of cheap goods, or, at least, of cheaper goods than the Western world can, in general, supply. Markets that could not be pried open with the bayonet may open more easily to peaceful Japanese trade. This, at least, has been the rule in the past history of Sino-Japanese trade, which tended to flourish in periods when "positive" policies were in abeyance.

It would seem essential that trade between China and Japan be encouraged to the limit of its natural development. There is no valid reason for barring cheaper Japanese goods from aiding in the large-scale program of economic reconstruction which China will be undertaking after the war. More than this will be required, however. In addition to China, the present colonial and semicolonial areas of Southeast Asia and India constitute natural markets for Japanese goods as well as natural sources for Japanese purchases of raw materials. It is vital, for the Western world as well as for Japan, that this vast underdeveloped area be given the chance to enter upon an unhampered program of industrial development that will support the advance of its various national entities toward full political independence. Few other issues in the postwar Far East outweigh this one in potential significance. Pledges, both specific and general, are already on the books. The Philippines has been promised full independence in the most concrete terms. More recently President Roosevelt stated that one of the principles which will guarantee an enduring peace involves "recognition of the rights of millions of people in the Far East to build up their own forms of self-government without molestation." While this principle was enunciated with particular reference to Japanese aggression, it is one that cuts both ways. Carried to fruition in the political sphere, and adequately implemented on the economic side, it can go far to provide an answer to the trade requirements of both Japan and the Western world in the postwar era.

It can hardly be doubted that the United Nations will give the most serious consideration to Japan's problem of economic self-support when peace is made. A graphic illustration of this problem can be supplied in terms of the rural and urban percentages in Japan's population. Accepting the Japanese militarists' plaint that the farm population has fallen to the 40 per cent minimum which they have set, the farmers now total about thirty millions. Urban areas probably contain well over 50 per cent of the total population. It must be admitted that the stimulus provided by war industries has mainly contributed to the rapid growth of the urban population in recent years. Excluding this factor, it remains true that the rural-urban migration has contributed to the soundness of Japan's economic structure. A declining rural population greatly facilitates achievement of the basic social adjustments required in the Japanese countryside. The postwar aid extended by the United Nations to Japan in the solution of its economic problem might well be conceived in terms of maintaining the present rural-urban ratio or even of increasing the numbers in urban areas. This aim would provide an objective measure of the extent to which sufficient trade opportunities had been made available to the Japanese. Provided opportunities of this scope were opened to Japan, it might also be possible to indicate that their continuance depended on the degree of achievement in liberalizing the Japanese regime along both political and economic lines. Success in affording Japan adequate means of self-support would obviously provide the staunchest bulwark to a liberal government and the strongest incentive to peaceful collaboration with the rest of the world.

It should be re-emphasized that, in the main, the Japanese people will have to carry out the above-mentioned changes themselves. The essential point is that we throw our influence behind those forces in Japanese life which will be interested in effectuating these reforms, and that we do not lend our support to those elements which will merely be trying to re-establish the old order on a somewhat refurbished basis. No one can predict the exact conditions which will exist in Japan at the end of the war. It is possible, but not at all certain, that a vast social revolutionary upheaval will occur, burning away in its fires much of the dross of old Japan. There would be no sound reason to view this phenomenon as an unmitigated calamity. If such conditions developed toward the end of the war, they would help to shorten its last stages. If they developed after defeat, they could perform many tasks which it would be less politic for us to impose in the peace terms. It would rather be the function of the United Nations to hold the ring while the issue is being settled by the Japanese, and then to seek immediate relations with the representatives of the new popular forces which had asserted their leadership, as Generalissimo Chiang Kai-shek has suggested.

It is necessary to end this analysis on a note of warning. There is no certainty that we shall have the will, the patience, or the skill adequate to guide Japan along new and better paths of development. But we should be forewarned that, if the old forces are permitted to re-establish themselves in Japan, it will be impossible for us to hold them in leading strings or to prevent them from amassing the power to strike again, first for their independence from our controls and then for domination. Their colonies may be lost, their navy sunk, their merchant marine destroyed, their military establishments dismantled, their foreign assets seized, reparations exacted. Germany suffered most or all of these calamities, too. On its home islands Japan will still possess a disciplined, hard-working, literate people of seventy-five millions. The labor power of these millions will rapidly re-create all the values taken away at the time of defeat. In ten or twenty or thirty years Japan will again be strong. With no changes in the social order, the reduced living standards of the workers and farmers enforced by the war will continue to exist after the war. The competition of Japan in world markets will be keener than ever. As Japan grows strong again, the desire for revenge will also develop. The militarists will spearhead another preparatory drive that will embrace the aristocracy, the industrialists, the landlords, and the financiers. Propaganda will be spread among the hungry and disillusioned workers and farmers, diverting their attention to foreign conquest as the way out of their misery and conditioning them for a new war. Disarmament regulations will not forever prevent the Japanese militarists from training their armies or the industrialists from making the latest types of munitions. The old forces can be replaced; they cannot be restored to power and then permanently curbed.

To break the cycle of aggression, the United Nations must devote their energy to aiding the Japanese people to find the new leadership that will give them a country having at least the substantial elements of political, economic, and social health. Once this is accomplished, it will not be difficult to fit Japan into the new world community which will be in construction at the same time.

REBUILDING A WAR-TORN WORLD

Francis B. Sayre

Diplomatic Adviser, United States Relief and Rehabilitation Administration

THE PROBLEM OF CIVILIAN RELIEF AND REHABILITATION IN the territories liberated from Axis control in Europe and Asia is an intensely practical one. To some this may seem far less important and exciting than, let us say, the future boundaries of the Soviet Union or the political postwar arrangements for keeping the peace. Perhaps so. But this is a problem which is actually confronting us now. We cannot sidestep it. Either we must meet it, open-eyed and prepared, and master it in the only way it can be mastered—by international planning and international co-operation and international action—or else we must admit failure and look to the future with sorry hearts and grave misgiving. But, believe me, we shall not fail. And our success in solving this particular problem will have a significance in our postwar peace work reaching far beyond the field of relief and rehabilitation.

I

We are fighting today to make secure for ourselves and for our children a way of life which is very precious to us—one based upon individual freedom, upon equality of opportunity and equal justice to the weak and to the strong. We are fighting to establish the supremacy of the rights of the common people. In political terms this means democracy; it means government resting upon the desire and the consent of the governed. It means the right of free speech and the right to freedom of conscience. In economic terms it means a system of free enterprise—free enterprise not, indeed, of the

87

nineteenth-century, *laissez-faire*, thoroughgoing type, not a chaotic freedom from all governmental restraint, but the power within the general framework of governmental control to organize and conduct and build up one's own work or business as one sees fit as long as one does not pursue anti-social ends. The rights of the common people, for which we are fighting, mean the right to a job and the right to a living wage. They mean economic as well as political security.

To win this way of life pious hopes and Fourth of July oratory will not be sufficient. Very clearly the first step for attaining these objectives must be the winning of the present war. Should we fail in this our whole economic system would have to be regimented from top to bottom to achieve military objectives. There could be no possibility of any kind of freedom of enterprise. There could be no possibility of individual liberty or stable peace.

But it is equally clear that the winning of the war will not be enough. After the military victories have been won, the more difficult part of the task will begin. And at the very threshold of the enormous work of rebuilding and reconstruction and regeneration, we face a preliminary problem that itself is of staggering proportions—the problem of bringing emergency relief and rehabilitation to peoples enslaved by Axis tyranny and destitute through Axis cruelty, of keeping them alive and assisting them to their feet so that they can once more take a hand in the world's work and help in the building of the new world for which we are fighting.

II

The shadow of human distress which hangs over great areas of the world today is black indeed. Never before in all history has humanity faced on a world-wide scale such stark need, such gripping destitution. In four years of fighting in Europe and six years of fighting in Asia, the Axis has overrun thirty-five nations in which were living over five hundred millions of people. It has looted and plundered and stripped them of their resources. It has disrupted their economies and their productive power. Nazi masters in some countries in Eastern Europe have cut the peoples' rations to less than one thousand calories a day, which is about a quarter of the ordinary American army ration. Thousands and thousands of men and women and children are being intentionally and systematically starved.

In spite of man's astounding recuperative powers this war has so shattered and undermined peacetime productive capacities in many areas as to make a quick convalescence impossible without organized assistance from the outside. Machines and equipment have deteriorated. Many factories are in ruins. Commerce is paralyzed. Railways and transport facilities have broken down. Fishing fleets have been destroyed. Lack of fertilizer has impaired the fertility of the soil. In Nazi-occupied Europe farmers have lost about one-fourth of their cattle and a third of their draft animals. We do not yet know what wholesale and ruthless destruction will be ordered by the Nazi command before they are finally driven out from the territories they at present occupy. But we do know that whole populations will be in acute distress and will need quick and effective help if we are to avoid the breakdown of civilization in many parts of Europe and Asia.

III

Three possible courses lie open to us, the people of the United States. The first is to ignore the problem and do nothing—to concentrate instead upon getting back to "normalcy." The second is to attempt to solve it singlehanded, with only American resources, so as to preserve our complete independence of action. The third is to join in a carefully planned, international enterprise in which all of the United Nations will contribute to the cost and co-operate in the work.

The first of these three courses is utterly impractical. We cannot ignore the problem even if we would. The men and women of America simply would not consent to see the people of the United Nations, by whose side we are fighting a common enemy and for a common cause, destitute and suffering and dying for lack of the things which we could send them.

Even were this not the fact, there are compelling reasons— military, economic, political—which would make a do-nothing policy suicidal.

Military necessity makes imperative protection and stability in the rear. Without adequate civilian relief work military operations and military supply lines would be constantly imperiled by civil disturbance or by epidemics. For a time following the entry of the United Nations troops civilian relief is a part of the military job.

After the active fighting is over the American people have, in the restoration and maintenance of political and economic stability, an equally large and important interest at stake. Our nation cannot remain prosperous in a world of bankrupt customers. We must help Europe and the Far East back onto their feet, for we have learned now that the United States cannot possibly maintain a healthy economy if Europe and Asia are on their backs. Our own economic interests demand at the earliest possible moment the restoration of functioning and stable economies in the war-torn areas of Europe and Asia.

From the long-range viewpoint the stake of the American people in civilian relief abroad is even more compelling. If after the war we allow hunger and disease and suffering to go unrelieved, black despair will be followed by chaos and rebellion and renewed fighting. We shall reap the whirlwind.

It is clear as crystal that the first course of action—doing nothing—is as dangerous as it is impractical.

If we are to be realistic, the second course of action—the United States trying to meet the relief problem alone—is equally impractical. It is fantastic to talk in terms of the United States, singlehanded, undertaking to feed and clothe and rehabilitate all the victims of the present war. There is not enough surplus food or supplies in all the United States to meet such a need. The task is too great and too complex to be met by any nation acting alone. Relief supplies must be produced and made available in many countries, both within and without the confines of the United Nations. In the light of the needs of all of the liberated countries, relief and rehabilitation goods from every quarter of the earth, if insufficient to meet the need, must be allocated as between the separate countries, liberated and to be liberated, and distributed accordingly; and this manifestly can be effected only by international machinery and through international control. Only through an organized international group in which every nation concerned participates is it possible to gain the willing and active support necessary for this monumental task.

IV

Such was the course which our government wisely chose to pursue. It took the leadership in drafting an agreement to set up such an international relief organization. In response to its invitation, delegates from forty-four nations, representing some eighty per cent of the people of the world, met together November 9, 1943, in the historic East Room of the White House and attached their signatures to the document setting up an international Relief and Rehabilitation Administration. The purposes and functions of the Administration, as defined in the agreement, are to plan, co-ordinate, and administer measures for the relief of victims of war through the provision of food, fuel, clothing, shelter, and other basic necessities; medical and other essential services; and to assist in the production and transportation of these articles in local areas, so far as necessary to the adequate provision of relief, in order to minimize the amount of necessary imports.

It was a new adventure. Never before had the peoples of the East and the West, the North and the South, met together to pool their resources and to organize themselves upon an international scale to help bind up the wounds of war, to assist in feeding the hungry, and to help care for the sick.

On the day following the signing the delegates of the forty-four nations took a special train to Atlantic City; and there they spent the next three weeks organizing the new United Nations Relief and Rehabilitation Administration—UNRRA, as it is called—and charting the course which it should follow.

Whenever people come together from the four corners of the earth, difficulties and differences of opinion are bound to arise. The Atlantic City conference was no exception. Even inconsequential differences kept arising to plague us. For instance, there was the question of language. Our original draft of the permanent rules provided that English should be the official language. The French pressed a motion that French should be added as an official language, and secured its adoption. Then the Latin American countries pressed for Spanish. The Brazilian delegates thereupon moved for Portuguese. Finally, the Russian rose to his feet and for ten minutes filled the air with ringing Russian oratory. Then we proceeded to reconsider. If we were to move forward, there was only one way that was practical. We went back to English as the single official language.

So it was throughout the conference. We did not see always eye to eye. But we were determined to get on with the business. We ironed out all differences and went forward. When after three weeks of intensive work the conference came to a close, it was triumphantly clear, as one of the delegates voicing the general thought expressed it, that "a milestone in international collaboration of freedom-loving nations" had been passed.

The structure of UNRRA is simple. The policy-making body is the council, composed of one representative for each of the forty-four member states. It meets not less than twice a year. It has appointed a number of standing and technical committees—a central committee, to determine emergency policies when the council itself is not sitting; a European and a Far Eastern committee, to advise and make recommendation on problems of relief and rehabilitation within those areas; a supplies committee, to advise the council and the director general on general policies regarding the provision, financing, and transport of supplies; a committee on financial control, to review the annual budgets and generally to advise the council on financial matters; and additional standing technical committees on agriculture, on displaced persons, on health, on industrial rehabilitation, and on welfare.

The executive authority of UNRRA lies in the director general, appointed by the council. His is a position of keystone importance; for, within the limits of available resources and the broad policies determined by the council, he has full power and authority for carrying out relief operations. In the broad scope of power thus vested in the executive, UNRRA goes beyond previous international organizations. At Atlantic City the council, by unanimous acclaim, chose as director general, Herbert H. Lehman, former governor of the state of New York. His choice as head of UNRRA is a singularly happy one. He is a man of tested ability, free of political and personal ambition and consecrated to the cause of humanity. Ever since he was called to Washington by President Roosevelt to take over the work of relief and rehabilitation operations, I have worked shoulder to shoulder with him, day in and day out, in the most intimate kind of contacts. I have utter confidence in his integrity of purpose, his ability, and his determination to get the job done.

Important policy determinations were reached at Atlantic City. One related to the scope of the work to be undertaken by UNRRA. As the various committees and subcommittees into which the council broke up studied the needs in the occupied countries, an appalling picture of hunger and disease, ruin and devastation, took shape before them. The light of civilization has burned alarmingly low. Millions of people have been all but submerged by the war. Nevertheless,

93

it has been clear from the very outset that, with the limited funds and supplies which it would be able to muster, UNRRA must strictly confine itself to meeting emergency needs during an emergency period. UNRRA cannot undertake the work of long-term reconstruction, important and essential as this task undoubtedly is. UNRRA's task will be to tide people over a critical period, not to build a new world for them.

On the other hand, UNRRA must not become a Santa Claus—must avoid putting peoples on the dole. UNRRA's real job will be to help people to help themselves, and enable them to produce their own relief goods. Success for UNRRA will consist in eliminating within the shortest possible time all need for its existence.

The council went out of its way to declare an unequivocal and uncompromising stand against every form of discrimination in the distribution of goods. There is always the danger that the distribution of relief goods be made the instrument for gaining political or other ulterior ends. Against any such practices UNRRA has declared unceasing war. "At no time shall relief and rehabilitation supplies be used as a political weapon," voted the council, "and no discrimination shall be made in the distribution of relief supplies because of race, creed, or political belief." Under this vote, whenever UNRRA undertakes to distribute or to arrange for the distribution of relief goods, it pledges all of its influence and power to ensure a distribution to individuals or to groups based solely on the criterion of human need.

The Atlantic City meeting made very clear that UNRRA is in no sense a world-wide charity organization. Those nations which are the fortunate possessors of sufficient foreign exchange to be able to pay for the relief goods which they need will be expected to do so. "It shall be the policy of the Administration," voted the Council, "not to deplete its available resources for the relief and rehabilitation of any areas whose government is in a position to pay with suitable means of foreign exchange." On the other hand, nations unable to pay will not for that reason be denied relief. Both as among liberated countries and as among various classes of the population within a country, the distribution of relief shall be based upon actual need and not upon ability to pay.

One of the encouraging aspects of Atlantic City was the fundamental unanimity of agreement, even with respect to such difficult and complex problems as the financing of relief. The council, measuring the well-nigh limitless needs as against such resources as it hoped might be made available, unanimously recommended that "each member government whose home territory has not been occupied by the enemy shall make a contribution for participation in the work of the Administration, approximately equivalent to one per cent of the national income of the country for the year ending June 30, 1943." This would mean a total sum set aside for relief and rehabilitation in the liberated territories amounting to between two and two-and-a-half billion dollars. Under the council's recommendation, up to ninety per cent of each state's contribution may be spent in purchases of its own products within its own borders. The invaded countries, having already contributed far more than their share in lives and blood and sacrifice, should, it was agreed, contribute to UNRRA whatever they could and not be asked for a one per cent contribution. As a matter of fact, these countries will themselves furnish the bulk of the relief and rehabilitation supplies which they need, and, whenever able, will pay for such goods as have to be brought in from the outside.

Into the formulation of plans at Atlantic City went the best thinking and experience of those who have worked upon kindred problems of meeting human need. The delegates realized that distribution of relief must be carried out in such a way as to avoid embarrassment or humiliation to the recipients. It is not a case of doling out charity to paupers but of helping to get back onto their own feet those who by their pluck and by their heroism have succeeded in surviving and surmounting Axis savagery.

We cannot buy Europe and Asia back to prosperity. Recovery can never be given away to passive peoples. Recovery can come only as a result of a people's own effort—as a result of the back-breaking work of rebuilding and restoring and remaking. Our part must be, in so far as we are worthy and are able, to help those who have been through the fire of heroic suffering to do that themselves.

V

Concretely, what will be the practical job of the United Nations Relief and Rehabilitation Administration?

Apart from Russia, the population of the eight Allied countries of Europe invaded by Germany, and of Denmark, is about 135 million. If Italy is added, the total becomes about 180 million. By no means all of these people will need to be fed after liberation. Most rural people, for example, will, we hope, be able to look after themselves. But of this number some 70 million will almost surely need supplemental food if they are to get even two thousand calories a day. Although the average person will get, perhaps, only about five hundred calories of supplemental food, the total required will be equivalent to feeding, say, 18 million people two thousand calories a day. These figures do not allow for damage which the enemy may do in his retreat. If he succeeds in scorching the earth generally, the requirements will be much greater. And remember that these figures do not include Russia or the Far East.

We cannot expect that people will be able to participate in the building of a constructive peace as long as they are disorganized and hungry and desperate. First things must come first. We must begin by binding up the wounds of the stricken and feeding the starving, by checking the ravages of epidemics and disease, by helping liberated peoples to replace anarchy by law and organized government.

All this we must do with an immediacy and on a scale never before attempted. During the initial stages, as already pointed out, responsibility for the work of civilian relief has been assumed by the Allied armies. The United Nations armies must prove welcome deliverers. They must preserve the loyalty of liberated populations so that supply lines will be safe from interruption and may be guarded with minimum forces. The armies must prevent the outbreak of disease or epidemics behind the lines for the protection of their own troops. We must get liberated areas at the earliest possible moment back onto their feet and producing so as to lessen the strain on military supplies.

As order is established in each of the liberated territories and as the troops move forward into more advanced areas, however, the military will want to relinquish these responsibilities and hand them over to civilian hands. UNRRA must then be prepared, when requested by the military or by whatever government is in control, to take over the job of civilian relief and rehabilitation.

In large outline, UNRRA in the discharge of its responsibilities will have a fourfold task: first, to build up adequate reservoirs of foodstuffs and other relief and rehabilitation supplies which it can tap as needs arise; second, to assure an equitable and efficient distribution of these among all the liberated populations; third, to assist distressed populations to produce their own relief supplies, thus ending, at the earliest moment possible, the need and expense of relief from the outside; and fourth, to assist in the care and, so far as possible, in the repatriation of displaced persons.

First as to the reservoir. Wheat, which is one of the most important food items, stands alone; for with wheat the main problem is lack of shipping rather than shortage of supply. Apart from wheat, however, the acute world shortages today make it impossible to buy relief and rehabilitation goods over the counter in sufficient quantity to meet postliberation needs. Each country has found it necessary to control and allocate, as among the various war needs and civilian needs, goods that are in short supply; and for this purpose national control agencies have been organized in the large producing countries. Consequently, UNRRA must work out arrangements with these national control agencies in the various countries and also with existing international control agencies, such as the Combined Boards, so that UNRRA can have available, as the need arises, specified quantities of stocks and stores.

In the light of the over-all needs for relief and rehabilitation supplies and of the available sources of supply both within and without the confines of the United Nations, UNRRA will have to work out careful plans to arrange for the acquisition or production of relief and rehabilitation goods within the various member states or elsewhere at such times and in such quantities as may prove necessary; and this it must do in ways which do not impede the effective prosecution of the war. UNRRA will, so to speak, maintain drawing accounts in forty or fifty different countries, drawing upon each of these accounts as the need may arise.

Second, there is the task of working out arrangements to assure an equitable distribution among all the liberated populations of such supplies as are available. If, for instance, a country with ample resources should buy up in world markets sufficient foodstuffs to feed its population on a standard of, perhaps, three thousand calories per person per day, the result would probably be a depletion of available world stocks of food supplies to a point which would not permit feeding the peoples of other countries up to a standard of, say, two thousand calories a day. As long as relief stocks are in acute short supply, some kind of international control must be exercised to ensure an equitable distribution based upon actual need rather than upon ability to pay. This means that UNRRA must plan well in advance the probable requirements of the liberated areas, country by country, and constantly keep correcting and checking these figures. At the same time it must be studying all available and potential sources of supply, keeping in constant touch and close communication with each of the member states. UNRRA must then assume the task of allocating as among the various liberated countries all relief and rehabilitation goods which are in short supply. This part of its task, manifestly, is in no way dependent upon whether relief goods are sold or given away.

A third part of UNRRA'S task will be what is known as rehabilitation. This means not merely helping people. It is better than that. It means helping people to help themselves. It reduces the need for supplies from the outside by assisting people to produce their own basic essentials. Its aim is to shorten the relief period, to economize on scarce supplies, and to end the necessity for emergency rationing. For instance, UNRRA will prefer to send in seed potatoes in time for planting rather than to ship potatoes for distribution all the next year. A shipload of fertilizer for impoverished soil may make half a dozen shiploads of food unnecessary a few months later. A few mobile repair units, some replacement parts for machines, and a bit of expert advice may help to get a power plant or a gas works into operation and thus enable a whole community of workers to get back into production and become self-supporting.

Still another part of UNRRA's tasks will have to do with the care and the repatriation of displaced persons. Today there are in Europe over twenty million people, in Asia a much larger number, driven from their homes by Axis armies or by the cruelties of war. Some are wandering and homeless, others enslaved in Axis labor gangs or imprisoned in concentration camps. Many of these people are weakened by hunger and disease. The problem of displaced and homeless persons, many of them in dire need, sick in body and in mind, will be one of the terrible and dreadful aftermaths of the war. The world has seldom, if ever, faced any problem of human woe comparable to it. It will be the task of UNRRA to assist in caring for these destitute refugees and, in so far as possible, in getting them back home.

VI

The cost of United States participation in the work of UNRRA is not large in comparison with the cost of our government's attempting to meet the need singlehanded or not meeting the need at all. During and after the first World War, when the United States undertook by itself to meet the cost of civilian relief work in Europe, the United States expended for relief some two and one-half billion dollars.

If, on the other hand, the United States in a burst of economy decided to close its eyes to the acute needs of Europe and Asia in the months ahead and to pursue the course of doing nothing, two consequences would be utterly inevitable. One would be the lengthening and protraction of a period of paralyzed and stagnant trade and business throughout the world. Following the war Europe and Asia will be in dire need of foodstuffs and cotton and automobiles, of textiles and agricultural implements and machinery, of the thousand and one things that the United States is prepared to produce in quantity and to sell—if only we can find markets and people with purchasing power to buy them. Each month of business prostration and economic paralysis in European and Asiatic markets would cost the American people literally hundreds of millions of dollars in idle factories, blighted export and import trade, mass unemployment, and lengthening bread lines. The second consequence, equally inevitable, would be the continuation of fighting after the armistice. In comparison with the cost of a third world war, the cost of relief operations is insignificant.

Americans who care about the future have a tremendous stake in the outcome of the Congressional debates.

VII

Millions of men and women all around the world, bleeding and suffering and starving for the cause of freedom and human justice, are today turning their faces in hope toward UNRRA. As the Chinese representative at Atlantic City put it:

The rivers of China, the roads of Russia, the streets of England, the fiords of Norway, the fields and cities of Belgium, of France, of Holland, the valleys of Yugoslavia and Greece, Pearl Harbor and the Coral Sea, have run with the blood and the tears of common men and women and children. We want the common man around the world who has felt this common suffering to know also a common healing and a common regeneration. . . . A great work lies ahead of us. Millions of freedom-loving people who suffered severely from aggression and hostilities look now to UNRRA with great hope.

The distressed people of Europe and Asia are not looking for charity. They have drunk deep of suffering, but many of them have gained thereby immeasurable strength and spiritual power. We who have not undergone such suffering look up to them in reverence and in gratitude. May I quote the words of Mr. Kerstens, the Netherlands minister of commerce, who represented that gallant nation at Atlantic City:

All Europe has been smashed and torn to pieces. Never before in the history of Europe has such a picture of horror and terror been seen. And yet Europe has not died. It has not even given in to the torturer. It has resisted from the first minute, and it will resist until the last second. What is the secret of this incredible strength? It is Europe's sense of civilization and freedom. The small continent from which the idea of human liberty has spread over the world refuses to die in the darkness of slavery. . . . The great periods of world progess are not those of material prosperity but those of spiritual strength, which is mostly won from suffering and sacrifice. The nations of Europe are vibrating with the desire to rebuild their lives and their countries. . . . They do not wait for any charity. They just wait for such amount of relief and rehabilitation as will be necessary to start things up again. Let us not fail them in their rightful expectations!

We shall not fail. Where there is the determined will to go forward in spite of seemingly insoluble problems and insuperable obstacles, nothing can stop human progress. We have that will. Backed by the solid support of the peoples of the world, we shall go forward, God willing, and help to bind up the wounds of war and build for a peace that will be enduring.

VIII

Before concluding I would stress one further thought. The hope of future peace depends upon how far the nations of the world can learn to work co-operatively for common ends—can learn the give and take which all genuine co-operation involves for the sake of gaining larger, more far-reaching objectives.

For months the armies in the field, perceiving that this was the only way forward, have been successfully learning and practicing this difficult lesson of international co-operation.

For months we back home have been talking about post-war planning and international collaboration. We have been discussing how to build sound foundations for a stable peace. Now we are facing the realities. UNRRA presents the acid test of whether we can or whether we cannot forget our selfish differences and work together, as our armed forces have done, wholeheartedly for common objectives which must be achieved if we are to go forward and attain humanity's place in the sun.

True, this is only part of the task which awaits us. Other more difficult parts of the work remain—the achievement of some form of international organization for the keeping of the peace, the effective limitation and control of armament production, the inauguration of practicable means for the peaceful settlement of international disputes, the reduction of trade barriers throughout the world, the elimination of unfair trade practices and discriminations, the development of international responsibility with respect to certain backward areas. Let us remember that these tasks cannot all be accomplished at once. Months and years of devoted study and consecrated effort will be necessary for the building of the international peace structure. Here, in this comparatively less difficult part of the task, we begin.

"UNRRA is the first great test," Governor Lehman recently declared, "of the capacity of the present world partnership of the United Nations and associated governments to achieve a peacetime goal. It represents a first bold attempt of the free peoples to develop efficient habits of working together. It is now up to all of us to prove that it is not only for war and destruction but also for help and healing that nations can be united to act for the common good. Then will peace have her victory no less than war."

CHINA, AMERICA'S PACIFIC ALLY

Y. C. YANG

*President of Soochow University and Director
of Speakers' Bureau of the Chinese News Service*

IF THE WORLD IS A STAGE AND LIFE A DRAMA, WE ARE CERTAINLY
at a most exciting moment in the mighty passing show of
world history. Momentous events of far-reaching consequences are taking place before our very eyes, involving not
only parts of the world but the whole of the globe, and
affecting the destiny not only of one age but of many generations to come.

If we were writing a review of this great scene in the
pageant of mankind, what should we put down as high points
in this colossal drama? Would we not, by common consent,
say that the first thing we should put down is that we are
now indeed living in the one-world era? If the moving finger
of time has done any skywriting at all, it is the announcement
that mankind has moved on from the stage of regional existence—be it the nation, the continent, or the hemisphere—
to the state of essential world unity. We are today facing a
world situation, with world problems which demand world-
wide solutions and call for world-wide co-operation. However our interest and devotion may be centered in our own
respective halls of independence, we have to bear in mind
that each and every one of them is located on the grand
concourse of interdependence. We are not only separate
entities but, at the same time, component parts of an in-
separable unity. The world is indeed a globe; and the globe,
as such, has neither sides nor faces, top nor bottom. It is an
integrated and indivisible whole.

We are, as it were, in the second great age of discovery. Columbus and the explorers of the fifteenth and sixteenth centuries made the great discovery that the world was much larger than the people then thought it to be; modern science, through improved mediums of communication and new means of transportation, and modern life, with all its connections, implications, and ramifications, have made the world, in effect, much smaller than we thought it to be.

With this change in the dominant characteristic of environment has also come a change in the central theme of life. If during the past few centuries human progress has been measured in terms of growth of individual liberty, for the next few centuries world progress will be rated according to improvements in community life and intercommunity relations. This fact of the unity of the world is the Maypole around which the nations of the world will have to dance. Whether the pattern woven at the top will be beautiful and symmetrical or not depends upon how well we can keep this point in mind and co-operate with each other in playing the game of life.

Not even such a general division of the world as that into the East and the West is possible or practicable. For, it is quite evident that the Far East is no longer far. Indeed, the East and the West are no longer separated nor separable from each other. They have met on the highway of the world and will go down the road of history together. If this was the great lesson which the West taught the East in the nineteenth century, the twentieth century is adding some footnotes to make clear that the same thing is equally true in the relations of the West to the East. If ever there was a time when it was true that "East is East, and West is West, and never the twain shall meet," it is certainly no longer true; for the West has met the East, and the East has met the West, and the twain never will again fall apart.

Now in this new world situation of growing unity and interdependence what are the respective positions of China and the United States—how are they related to the whole world and how to each other? These are certainly questions of direct, immediate interest which should engage our attention.

To start with, we may say that the United States of America is today occupying a central position of pivotal importance in world affairs. Geographically, you are the "midway island" in the highway of the world. Politically, you are the center of gravity in international relations. Culturally, you had roots in Europe and have spread fruits to Asia; and, as far as China is concerned, you are a most important link between European civilization and Oriental culture. Spiritually, you have time and again assumed a moral leadership in the world which many nations have been glad to follow.

From being somewhat detached from the other continents of the world, America today faces both Europe and Asia at the same time. It is like a huge building occupying an entire city block, having, shall we say, the "Atlantic Boulevard" on one side and the "Pacific Avenue" on the other. If, according to the traditional conception, your main, front street is on the Atlantic side, very few, perhaps, will now fail to appreciate that the street on the Pacific front is no longer a back alley of no significance; it also has become a busy thoroughfare of great importance. In fact, although we cannot lift the veil of time and look the future squarely in the face, the growing significance of Asia as a factor in the life of mankind and the increasing importance of the Pacific in the development of the world can perhaps be easily traced in the broad outline of the shape of things to come.

To America, Asia is its second front, whether we think in terms of this present global war or with reference to the future world peace. American world relations and foreign policy should perhaps be viewed as an ellipse constructed on two foci, one centering in the Atlantic and the other in the Pacific region. As England is always thought of as your natural partner in Europe, so China should be regarded as your logical ally in Asia, especially if we hope that culture is to be the basis of, and co-operation is to be the means for, the development of a permanent order of peace and harmony in the Pacific.

As to the position of China in this unfolding picture of new Asia, it is almost as easy to see that the emergence of China as a great modern democracy is perhaps the most outstanding event in the Far Eastern history of the twentieth century, as the development of Japan into a great military power was in the nineteenth century. It is quite apparent that the nature of Asia and its relation to the world will depend, to a very appreciable extent, upon the place and position which China will occupy in Asia. For instance, an Asia dominated by the aggressive militarism of imperialistic Japan will be quite different from an Asia in which the peace-loving, democratic China is the major center of cultural influence.

China and America have been close friends since the beginning of their intercourse with each other. This traditional friendship has been the "talk of the town" in the world. It is a beautiful flower in the field of international relations. This is not to say or claim that we are perfect, or that our relations have been perfect in every way. It is hardly to be expected that our views should have always exactly coincided, or that our interests should have always been exactly identical, although it is remarkably significant how often and to what extent this has been true. What is significant and important is the fact that we have actually got along so well with each other for such a long time, that we do have a friendly feeling and attitude toward each other, and that we do have faith and confidence in each other. Furthermore, we have continually tried to improve our relations, as is evidenced, on your part, in your spontaneous decision to give up extraterritorial rights in China and in the more recent repeal of the Chinese exclusion law.

Now this Sino-American friendship is truly unique and

significant in more than one respect. First of all, it is significant because it is so natural and so spontaneous. Both
sides seem to have accepted it as part of life without raising
any question as to its why or wherefore. American friendship for China is proverbial; Chinese cordiality to America
is unique. This friendship is not just an *entente cordiale* between two governments but a genuine love match between
two peoples. These words may sound a little sentimental; but
they are, nevertheless, essentially factual.

In addition to this broad base which ensures its stability,
Sino-American friendship also rests on a deep foundation of
cultural understanding which binds the two nations together
in good will and mutual appreciation. This is seen to be not
just a happy accident when we bear in mind that probably
more Christian missionaries have gone to China from America
than from any other country, and that to America, China
has sent more of her choice sons and daughters for advanced
education than to all other Western countries put together.
It is also most interesting to note that he Chinese and Americans are very much alike in many important respects. In spite
of the superficial differences in our physical appearance, in
languages, and in many of our customs and traditions, there
are in the higher realm of basic ideals and fundamental concepts of life many points of remarkable similarity and agreement between us. Thus, first, we are both democratic. It is
true that the Republic of China was not born until the
beginning of this century; but the spirit of China as expressed
in the life of the people—in their customs, traditions, and
institutions—has always been fundamentally democratic. Then
we are both peace-loving. Neither of us has ever sought to
build national greatness on military strength, but both of
us have rather striven to distinguish ourselves in cultural
achievements. Both of us also have great esteem for and
confidence in education. In China, as in America, education
is the "Lincoln Highway" to distinction and achievement.
We may not have used the expression "brain trust," but we

have always trusted in brains. Finally, we may also say that both of us have always believed in the common man. For over two thousand years the symbol and model of manhood in China has been Confucius, a common man, wearing no crown on his head and holding no saber in his hand—not a great emperor nor a great conqueror but a great scholar.

China and America are now allies. Co-operation between them is natural and logical. We are living in a time when the line of demarkation has never been so sharply drawn between peace-loving democracies on the one hand and totalitarian military powers on the other, and when the nations of the world have never been so clearly divided into two distinct camps. But such partnership is also indispensable and imperative. For do we not both face the Pacific, now steadily emerging into prominence and importance? Do we not both have the same interest in keeping this area safe for democracy, safe for its peaceful development, and safe for the growth of commercial intercourse? Do we not thus have common vital interests and common tasks? Is it an unwarranted exaggeration of self-importance or a frank facing of the plain facts of the situation to say that we have a common mission and a common destiny in the Pacific? The Pacific today is not a peaceful basin but a storm center. But in the close co-operation between the two sister republics facing the Pacific will be found a most potent factor in making and keeping it peaceful, with all its meaning for and effect upon the peace and security of the whole world.

As allies, the common problems before us are, of course, first, how to win this war—win it completely and speedily—and, secondly, how to win the peace—win it truly and permanently.

That ultimate victory is already assured to the United Nations, there is no doubt. That victory is just around the corner, we have been warned not to say too hastily or too lightly, especially in the present case; there are two corners involved, and we must push toward and around both corners before our task is completely done. It is, of course, quite natural that those in Europe like to see Europe cleared up first and that those in Asia would like to see Asia cleared up first. Whether Germany should be first crushed before heavy pressure be put on Japan, or whether Japan should be first eliminated so that our whole attention can be turned to Germany, or whether it is possible to deal with both of them at the same time, may be accepted as questions of high military strategy; but that both Germany and Japan should be thoroughly defeated so that neither of them can again become a military menace to the world and that the sooner the Far Eastern situation can be vigorously dealt with, the better it will be for the general cause of the United Nations, and the more economic in effort and sacrifices for all concerned, are questions about which there can be no difference of opinion.

Among the members of the United Nations, China has been in the war the longest.

Now, for more than six and one-half years, a titanic struggle has been going on in her country in which we find a colossal contest between a mighty military power, which conceives and boasts of its armed forces as being invincible, and a great peace-loving people who have been valiantly resisting them with a spirit which has shown itself to be indomitable. The whole war situation can, perhaps, be summed up in the one brief sentence: China has been bleeding painfully and profusely for a long time, but that bleeding China is today still standing erect, unyielding and uncompromising, with faith unimpaired and courage undaunted, not only more determined than ever before to defend her own national life and existence, but now, as a member of the United Nations, to contribute "all that we are and all that we have" to the common struggle "against the savage and brutal forces seeking to subjugate the world," so that lawless military aggression may be crushed and the principles of justice and righteousness be vindicated.

Pitched against a foe with a powerful war machine so

vastly superior to her own in modern military equipment, China's remarkably effective resistance has been a pleasant surprise to her friends, and a stunning astonishment to her enemy. Now what has given her this sustaining power? Mencius, the great disciple of Confucius, once said: "Life I desire, but there is something I desire more than life; death I detest, but there is something I detest more than death." Knowing that subjection to the sinister, pernicious forces now disturbing the world and against which we are fighting would mean not only the political domination and economic exploitation but the moral degradation and cultural disintegration of all who come under their power, and feeling that there is no way out except through the valley of the shadow of death if we are ever to come to the mountain top to enjoy the sunshine of freedom and breathe the air of liberty, the Chinese have been ready to face death in order to find life, in the spirit so well described by Mencius. Here, in this spirit of heroic resistance, we may perhaps hear a distant echo of that famous American exclamation, "Give me liberty, or give me death!" so expressive of the spirit which made the American War of Independence such a glorious success. Then the Chinese have been taught for ages to live in implicit faith that, in spite of violence and wickedness, the world is after all a moral order in which there is a God or Providence which rules over and can overrule men. There is a well-known Chinese proverb which says that "those who are with Heaven prosper, and those who are against Heaven perish." If the Chinese were superstitious, this faith in the moral order of the universe is certainly one of their abiding "superstitions." Many Chinese also foresaw, from the very beginning, that in the Sino-Japanese conflict were involved general principles and fundamental issues of such importance and with such far-reaching consequences that the rational and enlightened in the world would sooner or later understand that "our cause is the cause of mankind" and would eventually make common cause with us.

111

Now when can we say that the war shall have been truly and fully won? Victory, in the fuller and deeper sense, calls not only for the military defeat of the enemies but also for the settling of some well-defined issues and the attainment of certain definite objectives. What are we fighting for? What are our war aims?

Is it not true that we are each fighting, first of all, in defense of the manhood of our nation, whether we interpret this to mean national life and independence or national honor and vital interests? As there is such a thing as the manhood of the individual, so there is also such a thing as the manhood of the nation. And shall we go a step further and say that there is also such a thing as the manhood of humanity itself, which the United Nations are now united in defending? And, if we bear in mind that man is created in the image of God, then the defense and preservation of the manhood of humanity would mean that we must fight against all forces which may degrade man from that exalted state or deface that perfect image.

In the second place, are we not all agreed that we are fighting to preserve and protect the democratic way of life? We are fighting "that government of the people, by the people, for the people" shall not perish from the face of the earth. But, if the democratic way is accepted as the true way of life, then should we not do more than just fight for its preservation? Should we not also seek, in a more positive way, to extend its spirit and principles to the whole world and into the sphere of intercommunity life, as it has already been accepted in the intracommunity life of mankind, so that this democratic principle will be made applicable to international relations as well as to individual relations?

Then, in the third place, do we not say that we are fighting to preserve certain spiritual values of life? Is it not true that in the present world conflict are involved not only questions of material interest and territorial possessions, the fortune and future of nations, but also certain fundamental concepts of life and basic principles of human relationship—the status of the individual, the dignity of personality, the ends of government, the basis of international relations, and even the place which man will give to God and religion in society? In the truest and fullest sense, therefore, really to win the war means that these fundamental ideas and objectives should be clearly defined and the lofty principles outlined in the Atlantic Charter, in the Four Freedoms, in the Declaration of the United Nations, and the statements issued after the Moscow, Cairo, and Teheran conferences, must be fully and faithfully executed. Here is a spiritual front of the war which must receive proper attention if we really want to see the future course of history and civilization make a turn for the better.

But to win the war is not the end in itself; rather, it is only the means to the end. One of the encouraging things in the present situation is the fact that peace and postwar problems are receiving much earlier and much more serious attention now than was the case at the time of the first World War. *V* will stand for complete victory only when it is regarded as an opening wedge to a new era of real, durable peace. War will not last forever; peace of some sort we shall have in any case; but it makes all the difference in the world, and to the world, what kind of peace we will make, and the type of postwar order we will establish. The coming peace will answer the question whether the billions of dollars we are spending for the war and the millions of men we are throwing into the battlefields are sacrifices worth the price. It will also determine whether the world will continue in a state of perpetual unstable equilibrium or whether it can be lifted to a more stable foundation of peace and security.

A real, durable peace must fulfill at least two essential conditions. First, it must be just in principle; and, second, it must be world-wide in scope. A peace which is not essentially just and righteous is defective in quality standard,

113

and one which is not world-wide in its conception and application is deficient in quantity content.

But what is a just peace? Shall we say that a just peace is one which is not dominated by the spirit of unrestrained vengeance, nor unduly influenced by indulgent condonation? God is love, but is not God also just and righteous? Should we not say that Christianity is not love in place of justice—but rather love in addition to justice? In traditional Chinese moral and political philosophy love and justice were always mentioned together; the benevolent attitude was justice seasoned with love. But, after all and above all, is not the justice we should keep in mind the justice and right of humanity itself, and of the future generations to come? These are the primary considerations to which we should give careful attention in our effort to make a real, just, and durable peace.

Now what is a world peace? Shall we say that it is one in the formulation of which the general welfare of humanity and the fundamental requirements of world security are given first priority? A postwar world resting upon group interests and regional arrangements which do not themselves rest on a broad world basis nor fit into some sort of world organization cannot stand the test of time and will likely be just another armistice. Any settlement based primarily upon group interests will be like a table standing on legs of uneven length. Any postwar order less than world-wide will be like a body in the shape of an inverted pyramid, standing on its smaller end.

There are persons who would say that, human nature being what it is, any world organization for collective security is simply impossible and impracticable. But does not the whole history of the evolution of political organization—the development of human society from the family to the clan, the clan to the city state, and the city state to the nation—point to some world organization as the next logical step in this same process of evolution, unless we should insist that mankind has, for some inexplicable reason, come to a state of arrested development when nationality or statehood has been attained? Whatever the theoretical arguments pro or con, a world organization is a practical necessity in this day of global contacts and global intercourse. To keep order and maintain security as well as to promote peaceful and profitable intercourse, every community must have some sort of organized control commensurate with the size of the community itself. Is not the successful formation of the United States of America out of the original thirteen states a sample of what is needed in the world today and an indication of the direction in which the nations should be definitely and progressively, even if it must be slowly, moving? The United nations must remain united in the coming age of peace, as they are now united in the war we are fighting, in a determined effort to work out some effective world organization for maintaining order and administering justice. Thus and thus only can we win the peace in such a way that those who die on the battlefield this time shall not have died in vain! Thus and thus only can the Golden Age of the world, which the Chinese have so long been dreaming of—a Grand Commonwealth of Harmony and Concord—be gradually realized! Thus and thus only can a beginning be made to translate into living reality the gospel news and bold proclamation which heralded the coming of the Prince of Peace, "Glory to God in the highest, and on earth peace, good will toward men"!

PROBLEMS OF THE SMALL STATES IN THE POSTWAR WORLD

VERA MICHELES DEAN

Research Director, Foreign Policy Association

WHAT MAKES A STATE GREAT OR SMALL IN THE MODERN world?

There are certain basic criteria of the power of nations—territory, population, and natural resources. Judged by these atributes, certain states can be classified as great and others as small. But if we should judge the greatness of nations by nonmaterial standards, we might classify small states in another category. True, Belgium, Czechoslovakia, and Greece, to name only a few small states, proved unable to defend themselves against attack by a great power. But shall we therefore say that they have no right to exist, just because they cannot defend themselves against aggression? Great powers, too, cannot always defend themselves. The reports issued by the Army and Navy of the atrocities committed by the Japanese in the Philippines is an old story to most small states. It is shocking to us because we are a great power. But it is equally shocking that far greater atrocities should have been perpetrated by the Japanese in China, by the Germans in conquered Europe. The fact is that great powers—Britain, Russia, China, the United States—have not proved more successful than small countries in defending themselves alone against aggression. And that is something we must constantly bear in mind before we pass glib judgments on the future of the small states.

But let us consider the nonmaterial standards as to whether a nation is great or small—let us consider the contributions

116

various nations have made to human civilization. In this period of global war it is inevitable that we should be thinking largely of the contributions states make in terms of material power—not only military power, but also industrial power—of the ability of countries to mobilize their raw materials and translate them through their industrial plants into effective armaments. In terms of material power many small states must be regarded as still small. But civilization is not advanced by industrial or military power alone. At certain critical junctures civilization may have to be saved by industrial or military power, as is happening today; but it is certainly not promoted by power used for purposes of destruction. If we are thinking in constructive terms, then many small nations may prove, in the long view of history, to be in truth greater than many of the so-called great powers. That is why it is so important today to re-examine small states in the light of the lessons we have learned in this war.

There are two lessons which I hope we can carry out of this war, because they will determine the future relationship between great and small powers. The first lesson, which we have already grasped, is that no nation—no matter how rich or powerful—can win the war alone. Neither Britain, nor the United States, nor Russia, nor China, despite great resources, has been able to win the war alone. From this lesson we must draw the corollary that no nation—no matter how rich or powerful—will win the peace alone. To win the peace, just as to win the war, all nations, great and small, will have to work together. The second lesson—which is very difficult for great states to learn—is that power must not be divorced from a sense of responsibility for the use of that power. There is no doubt that at the end of this war the great states which are victorious—Britain, the United States, Russia, and China—will emerge with their power increased manyfold as a result of the conflict. This may prove very good for the world, provided the great states use their enhanced power with a sense of responsibility for the international community. But it can also prove disastrous if the great states use their power irresponsibly, without consideration for weaker nations. We must hope that the peoples of the great states—the British, Russians, Chinese, and Americans—will learn how to conduct themselves responsibly in their relations to other countries. This depends not only on governments but on the peoples themselves. There is a dangerous tendency on the part of people who are citizens of great powers to look down on small nations and to disregard or flout their interests.

The crucial problem in the relations that are developing between small and great nations is that of discovering how we can combine security for all with a measure of independence for all. It is essential that both elements should be present in the international society of the future. It might, of course, be entirely possible for great powers to give security to small countries on their own terms. Russia, for example, could establish a sphere of influence in the Balkans; Britain could do the same for Western Europe; and the United States could strengthen its sphere of influence in the Western Hemisphere. Field Marshal Smuts, one of the staunchest supporters of the League of Nations, has recently stated that Russia will probably have a sphere of influence in Eastern Europe and the Balkans, and the United States in the Western Hemisphere, and therefore urged Britain to develop its own sphere of influence in Western Europe. A similar view in another form was expressed by Lord Halifax in Canada when he urged the British Dominions to tighten their foreign policy and defense bonds with Britain in the British Commonwealth of Nations. Incidentally, when we talk of small countries, we are not talking only of European nations. Canada, with a population of eleven million, is a small nation, just as Poland, with a population of forty million, and Czechoslovakia, with a population of fifteen million, are small nations.

The great powers, then, could give a measure of security
118

to the small countries as a sort of charitable handout. But while small countries want security, they do not want it at the sacrifice of what they regard as their independence. They do not want to be treated as mere satellites or appendages of the great powers. Here we come to the critical difficulty involved in the relationship between great and small states. The small countries know that they cannot preserve their territorial or economic independence in the future any more than they have in the past. But, rather than be tied down to a regional setup in which they would have to acquiesce in the demands of adjoining great powers, they would prefer to become members of an international organization on terms of equality with the great powers. Every small nation realizes that we can no longer live in a world of small, closed units. Our international political institutions— the nation-states with their panoply of sovereignty—were formed in the seventeenth and eighteenth centuries when the national state was founded on the divine right of kings, a right since then transformed into the divine right of sovereign states. Yet economically, technologically, and psychologically we have moved to a much more spacious concept of relations between nations. Today we can span the world by radio in a few minutes, by airplane in a few hours. Yet when we travel or trade across national frontiers we run into innumerable restrictions in terms of tariffs and other barriers to the circulation of people, goods, and ideas. Economic progress and technological advancement have not been shared by all countries, because political blockages still prevent such sharing. Today most people concerned with postwar reconstruction hope that, after the war, we will break down such barriers, that we will bring our political institutions into harmony with our economic and technological advancement.

At the same time we must not jump to the other extreme, thinking that, because the world has become interdependent, therefore we must bring all small states into the framework of already existing large units—notably the U.S.S.R., the United States, the British Commonwealth of Nations. True, the small states might benefit by inclusion in any one of these large units. But we cannot brutally coerce the small states against their will. That is what Hitler unsuccessfully tried to do. In his effort to build a new German empire on the European continent he sought to subordinate the small nations politically and economically to the German "master race" within the confines of his "new order." Yet for four years the people of the small nations of Europe have struggled against this "new order." They have not done so in order merely to bow to some new order devised by Russia, Britain, and the United States at the close of this war, which, in any case, cannot be won without their co-operation. If they did not accept a system imposed on them by Hitler through force and violence, they are not going to be in a mood to accept the more benevolent, but still definitely tangible, dictation of the great Allied nations.

We should be prepared for this and not be shocked or disillusioned when we find that the small countries want to have a share in the shaping of the postwar world. They have a right to expect such a share, for they have played an important part in moulding the civilization we are fighting to preserve. If we call the roll of the small countries of Europe, we remember immediately how much they have done for the world. The Scandinavian peoples, the Czechs, the Greeks, the Dutch, the Poles—when we call their names, we realize what they have contributed in terms of art, music, literature, and, most of all, in that struggle for human liberty in which we are once more engaged. To try to obliterate their identity would be to impoverish human civilization. On the other hand, it is natural for the great powers to feel that they cannot work responsibly with the small countries unless the small countries, in turn, take a responsible view of their international obligations and do not make use of their weakness to increase world anarchy.

120

This is one of the problems raised by the doctrine of self-determination. This doctrine found widespread acceptance in 1918. At that time large territorial units—the German Empire, the Austro-Hungarian Empire, the Russian Empire—were in a state of disintegration. All of these empires broke up because various national groups that had been integrated into them by force over the centuries saw in World War I an opportunity to break away and become independent. The doctrine of self-determination of nations is a corollary of freedom of the vote within our own nation. If every individual has a right to decide what party he will belong to, why should not national groups decide what state they will join or form? This is a convincing and appealing doctrine. But it was carried to absurd lengths after World War I because what people did not grasp at the time, and what we must understand now, is that a national group can attain most of the things that make life for its members worth living without necessarily forming a territorial national state.

What are the things that make a nation a cultural entity? The opportunity to speak its own language, to practice the prevailing religious beliefs, to follow the customs and traditions that are the essence of the national ethos. These things are far more important to the average human being than boundary stones, tariffs, or other items that form the usual subject matter of diplomatic conferences. What the doctrine of self-determination in practice failed to do was to recognize that national groups could achieve these values without breaking up whole areas of Europe into tiny territorial units, each striving vainly to build up political and economic security by its own efforts. If self-determination is pressed to its logical conclusion, then not only should the Poles have a national state but Czechs and Slovaks should not have been joined into one nation. Instead, each of the two groups should have had a state of its own. The Germans used this principle against Czechoslovakia and set up a state of Slovakia. Then, too, Croats, Serbs, and Slovenes should not have

121

been brought together in Yugoslavia. There is also no reason why there should not be an independent Ukraine. The Ukrainians, forty million strong, have been scattered between Poland and Russia, and their separation has long been a bone of contention in Russo-Polish relations.

But to break up Eastern Europe and the Balkans further would spell suicide for the small national groups. This is an area that has been swept by many tides of migration, where it is impossible, in consequence, to trace a frontier satisfactory to all concerned. If we began to ensconce each national group in its own territorial state, then we would have many more small states like Latvia, Estonia, and Lithuania, with populations of a million, or a million and a half, or two million, each trying to maintain its independence. It would be just as if each of our states should try to become an independent state, with its own tariffs and its own ambassadors abroad. This would not only be expensive for each state of our Union but also disadvantageous to all the other states. Yet that was the direction in which self-determination was taking Eastern Europe and the Balkans during the interwar years.

So the doctrine of self-determination must be reviewed today if we are to establish satisfactory relations between small and great states. Great powers always tend to use their influence on small countries with respect to such matters as frontiers and internal affairs. The chief difficulty between Poland and Russia is due not so much to territorial conflicts —Russia's proposal of the Curzon Line was essentially fair— but to the fact that Russia tried to oust the government-in-exile of Poland and replace it by a group of Poles formed on Russian soil. The United States and Britain, too, have tried to influence small countries. It was the threat of economic action on the part of Britain and the United States that forced Argentina to break off with the Axis. And our suspension of oil shipments to Spain from the Caribbean was used to persuade Spain to suspend the sale of strategic raw materials to

Germany. There is nothing new in this. As long as we live in a condition of international anarchy, small states are at the mercy of great powers. It can seldom be said that small nations start wars. Wars start because two or more great powers are in conflict about the territories or resources of small states.

What country was guilty of starting the war in 1914? Some people think that the action of Serbia precipitated that war. But small countries, on the whole, have been the objects, not the subjects, of international relations. They have been at the mercy of neighboring great powers; and unless we proceed to build an international organization during this war, small nations will remain vulnerable to great-power pressures in the future. If we are to avert this situation, we must create a framework within which great powers can work with small states on a basis of co-operation, and free from coercion. Within that framework it would be entirely possible, over the years, to create machinery that would assure the small countries the preservation of those values which are important to their peoples—their national spirit and heritage —and, at the same time, assure all nations a modicum of security and economic stability. This can be done through a dictatorship, as shown by the U. S. S. R., where 150 different races and nationalities have been given a measure of cultural autonomy yet have been welded together by a highly centralized political and economic system. The British Commonwealth of Nations offers another possible framework, based on democratic practices, where countries not equal in power are brought together on terms of equality.

But whatever machinery is set up to effect co-operation between great powers and small, it will have to be international, not regional, in character if it is to prove effective. Small countries cannot find security merely by forming blocs or customs unions among themselves. The Scandinavian bloc and others like it did not achieve security for their members. To believe that this method would succeed in the future is a dangerous mirage. What weak countries do when they come together is to pool their weaknesses; and that does not add up to the strength the small countries need if they are to resist the economic, political, and military pressures of great powers. Only in an international organization will small nations be able to stand up for themselves with the assurance that they can appeal for sympathy and support to their fellow citizens of the world community.

This was clearly shown by the United Nations Relief and Rehabilitation Conference held at Atlantic City in November, 1943. Up to that time small countries had been observers, not participants, of the discussions on military and political strategy held by the Big Four from Casablanca to Teheran. The small nations understood the necessity of big-power conferences, but they did not want to be excluded from decisions concerning the use the United Nations will make of victory. The small nations came to Atlantic City fearful of the plans of the great powers, but they began to feel reassured when they found that at least they had the opportunity to speak frankly about burning issues in an international forum in the presence both of other weak countries and of the great powers. In the light of this experience is seems essential that, in the midst of war, without waiting for peace, the United Nations should create a political council that would embrace all nations, large and small. There is no need for an elaborate constitution of world government. The Atlantic City conference was regarded by many who attended it as one of the most successful gatherings of the last twenty-five years. Yet its machinery was very simple. We could have similarly simple machinery for a Council of the United Nations. If the will to work together exists, it will be translated sooner or later into the necessary machinery and documents. The will to work together is essential if we are to collaborate on the countless problems that face us, especially in Europe, where there are so many small and weak nations—nations at the same time richly endowed for the development of world civilization.

So far there has been a crucial conflict between Russia, Britain, and the United States concerning the future political complexion of Europe. These three great powers must agree about Europe if the Continent is to be reconstructed. The conflict boils down to this. Many small nations see in Russia a possible champion of change and progress after the war, while in the United States they see a possible champion of restoration and even of reaction in Europe. Our policy in North Africa and Italy, justified though it may have been by military considerations, has not assured Europe that the United States will act as a proponent of democracy abroad. This divergence between the three great powers need not develop into a conflict after the war. On the contrary, it could be an honorable competition as to which way of life—Russian or Anglo-American—will seem best adapted to the internal needs of the small nations, which vary so widely in their economic and social development. It may be doubted that the Russian pattern is desired by the countries of Western Europe which had achieved political maturity and social and economic progress before 1939. But the Russian pattern may prove helpful for the countries of Eastern Europe and the Balkans whose prewar political, social, and economic conditions in many cases resembled those of Russia in 1917. One thing is clear. No attempt at reconstruction will prove long-lived unless the three great powers win the collaboration of small countries, which must share in the making of the peace as they have shared in the waging of the war.

A POSTWAR WORLD ORGANIZATION
FOR PEACE

HENRY A. ATKINSON

*General Secretary, The Church Peace Union and
The World Alliance for International Friendship Through the Churches*

WE CANNOT WIN THE PEACE UNLESS WE WIN THE WAR, BUT on the other hand we cannot win the war unless we also win the peace. With the cessation of hostilities there will come a lessening of the enthusiasm and idealism which are now carrying us on to victory. The principles enunciated in the Atlantic Charter have been agreed upon by practically all free peoples everywhere and are now accepted as the basis of agreement among the United Nations. The conferences at Moscow, Cairo, and Teheran clarified these principles and made more definite the plans and purposes for which we are fighting. These agreements must be given validity by the overwhelming approval and support of the United States. If we could have a vote now, a large majority of our people would sanction these principles; but when the war is over many will, because of political exigencies, fall victims to the appeal of selfish isolationism, and will repudiate them with the same facility with which they at present are accepted. We must guard against such an eventuality by a united effort to influence public opinion throughout the country strongly enough to secure agreement, before the end of the war, that America this time will stand by the rest of the world and take her full share of responsibility in policing the world, in helping to bring about necessary economic adjustments and the creation of a world-wide educational system to prepare

126

men and women in all nations, including our own, to live up to the ideals and responsibilities of world citizenship.

Comparing the present period with a similar period in the progress of the last war, we find that we are very much farther ahead now. We know this time what we are fighting for. We know the foes we face; we know the menace to our liberties; and we realize what defeat would mean. Most of us also realize that this war, in large part, grew out of the failure of our own nation to do its part at the end of the last war. The horrors through which we are passing at present have stabbed our consciences into a realization of these failures. We must not fail again. Recent polls indicate that the American people want their representatives in Congress to help provide the necessary machinery, in co-operation with the other nations, to make aggression impossible. There may be wide differences of opinion as to the type of world organization needed, but there is no difference of opinion in regard to our hatred for war and our determination at whatever cost to be free from its menace forever. Our Congress has responded to this universal demand from the country by passing the Fulbright Resolution in the House of Representatives and the Connally Resolution in the Senate. Thus, we put an end to American isolationism by taking the road to effective world co-operation.

Literally hundreds of various groups are studying the problems of peace. The United States Chamber of Commerce has set up an efficient organization, and its report is very illuminating. Out of almost two thousand local chambers of commerce, all except nine voted for American participation in some form of world organization to make our nation and the world secure from recurring war. Both the American Federation of Labor and the Congress of Industrial Organizations have strong committees studying these issues. The churches of the country are aroused. Sometime ago the Commission to Study the Bases of a Just and Durable Peace, of the Federal Council of the Churches of Christ in America, formulated a statement that was published under the title *Six Pillars of Peace*. This, with accompanying pamphlets, forms the basis of study in thousands of churches and other groups throughout the nation. The Federal Council also sponsored a nation-wide campaign under the title "The Christian Mission on World Order." One-day meetings were held in hundreds of cities, and through the influence of this mission many new groups began a serious study of these issues.

Under the direction of the Council of Bishops of The Methodist Church there was conducted throughout the country a "Crusade for a New World Order." Conferences and mass meetings were held in nearly one hundred communities with an attendance of over two hundred thousand persons.

Probably the most significant and comprehensive statement made by any of the religious groups was the *Pattern for Peace*.[1] This interfaith document was signed for the Catholics by Archbishop Edward Mooney of Detroit, Archbishop Samuel A. Stritch of Chicago, Bishop Karl J. Alter of Toledo, and forty-four of the highest prelates and officials of the Catholic Church in the United States. The signers for the Protestants were Bishop Henry St. George Tucker, President of the Federal Council of the Churches of Christ in America; Dr. Henry S. Coffin, Moderator of the General Assembly of the Presbyterian Church, U.S.A.; Bishop G. Bromley Oxnam of The Methodist Church; and forty-seven additional highest officials in all the Protestant denominations. For the Jews the signers were Dr. Israel Goldstein, President of the Synagogue Council of America; Dr. Louis Finkelstein, President of the Jewish Theological Seminary; Dr. Julian Morgenstern, President of Hebrew Union College; together with forty-seven other prominent rabbis and officials of the Jewish fellowship.

What adds particular significance to this declaration is that all the principles are based on direct quotations from the

[1] This document can be secured through the office of the Church Peace Union, 70 Fifth Ave., New York 11, N. Y.

official pronouncements of the highest ecclesiastical authorities, Jewish, Catholic, and Protestant.

The document embraces seven principles, which are stated as follows:

The moral law must govern world order

1. The organization of a just peace depends upon practical recognition of the fact that not only individuals but nations, states and international society are subject to the sovereignty of God and to the moral law which comes from God.

The rights of the individual must be assured

2. The dignity of the human person as the image of God must be set forth in all its essential implications in an international declaration of rights and be vindicated by the positive action of national governments and international organizations. States as well as individuals must repudiate racial, religious or other discrimination in violation of those rights.

The rights of oppressed, weak or colonial peoples must be protected

3. The right of all peoples, large and small, subject to the good of the organized world community, must be safeguarded within the framework of collective security. The progress of undeveloped, colonial or oppressed peoples toward political responsibility must be the object of international concern.

The rights of minorities must be secured

4. National governments and international organization must respect and guarantee the rights of ethic, religious and cultural minorities to economic livelihood, to equal opportunity for educational and cultural development, and to political equality.

International institutions to maintain peace with justice must be organized

5. An enduring peace requires the organization of international institutions which will develop a body of international law; guarantee the faithful fulfillment of international obligations, and revise them when necessary; assure collective security by drastic limitation and continuing control of armaments, compulsory arbitration and adjudication of controversies, and the use when necessary of adequate sanctions to enforce the law.

International co-operation must be developed

6. International economic collaboration to assist all states to provide an adequate standard of living for their citizens must replace the present economic monopoly and exploitation of natural resources for privileged groups and states.

A just social order within each state must be achieved

7. Since the harmony and well-being of the world community are intimately bound up with the internal equilibrium and social order of the individual states, steps must be taken to provide for the security of the family, the collaboration of all groups and classes in the interest of the common good, a standard of living adequate for self-development and family life, decent conditions of work, and participation by labor in decisions affecting its welfare.

In all of these studies and in all these pronouncements there is fundamental agreement that any organization of the world must prevent armed aggression, maintain peace with justice, and safeguard human rights.

The Commission to Study the Organization of Peace, under the chairmanship of Dr. James T. Shotwell, says in the introduction to the commission's fourth report:

Security, welfare and justice are the pillars of the world order for which we fight. They embody the hopes and dreams of countless millions of ordinary folk who yearn for a world in which their children may grow up free from the fears (and from the costs and consequences) of recurrent wars. This is what is meant by "security"—freedom from the fear of aggressive war.

They look also for a world in which new avenues of productive employment and economic opportunity may be opened up. This is what is meant by "welfare," using that word in its true and original sense of well-being.

Finally they look for a world in which international violence shall give place to the orderly processes of justice under law, including the safeguarding of human rights, a world in which men may be free to speak and worship as their conscience dictates. This is what is meant by "justice."

sick, destitute, cold, and homeless; never was there so much devastation and ruin. The task that will face the victorious governments and the Allied armies will be as great as, if not greater than, the task of winning the victory on the battle-field.

There are four steps that must be taken in the process of reconstruction—steps for which plans are now being made:

1. Relief and rehabilitation
2. Establishment of law and order
3. Reconstitution of the political life in the Axis nations as well as the occupied and Axis-controlled nations
4. Establishment of an authoritative political international organization

The immediate and most pressing demand will be for food and medicine. Starving populations are not amenable to reason. In all these nations the people are hungry, sick, discouraged, and without hope. Their primary need is food; and, with the allotment of bread and the promise of more to come, they will realize, even those in the enemy countries, that there are friends in the world and that there is hope in the future. Forty-four nations sent delegates to the United Nations conference held at Atlantic City, where plans were made for carrying on a wide program of relief and rehabilitation. An organization was set up, known as the United Nations Relief and Rehabilitation Administration, with the Hon. Herbert Lehman as director. Machinery for carrying out its program has been created by the United Nations, and all member nations have been asked to contribute one per cent of their annual budget as an initial fund for this important work. Plans are under way in Washington for our own government to contribute its share of thirteen hundred million dollars.

Beyond the immediate steps that UNRRA will undertake, there are more difficult problems to solve, such as the rebuilding of devastated cities, the reconversion of a war economy to peace ends, the establishment of new economic and social relations so as to secure more justice and avoid friction that lead to disputes and war. In other words, the task that faces the United Nations is to feed and supply the pressing needs of the peoples; then give them a chance to rebuild their lives, their homes, their cities, and re-establish their civilization on a new foundation.

Law and order must be established. The underground movements in the invaded nations have helped to maintain the courage of the people in their valiant struggle against the oppressors, toward whom they have naturally developed an intense hatred. A friend said to me some months ago in Pittsburgh: "Each of my friends in Poland has sworn that when the war ends five German heads shall roll in retribution for each Polish life lost." It is probably true that the same idea inspired by the same motives could be found among a large number of people in France, Belgium, Norway, and in other occupied nations. This is understandable and it is human, but individual vengeance is a dangerous thing and inevitably leads to anarchy and more bloodshed. The reign of terror that came in the wake of the French Revolution set back the cause of liberty for generations. A possible reign of terror, therefore, must be prevented.

With law and order established, the next step will be to help the people re-establish their own governments. There will be political difficulties in every nation, not only in Germany, Italy, and Japan, but among the nations that are now maintaining their governments in exile. Boundary disputes and questions of precedence are sure to arise. Party politics will emerge into sharpened conflict. But the people themselves within each country must be given the opportunity to decide by popular vote the kind of government they want.

The final step in this process will be to set up an authoritative international political organization. The various international conferences on labor, money and banking, and other matters, are all part of the process by which this world organization is being created. As time goes on and the nations hold their elections and establish their governments, they will be admitted as members of the United Nations. There must be formulated an international "Bill of Rights" which will become the basis of membership in the international organization. This declaration should embody the fundamental principles generally accepted as a minimum standard of decency on the part of the nations in their dealings with each other. This must also be made to apply to the treatment of peoples within each nation.

It is readily understood that these four steps cannot be taken in chronological order. One of our greatest difficulties will be that most of these issues will have to be faced at once and dealt with simultaneously. The point I wish to emphasize is that in organizing the world for relief and reconstruction, and for building up an international organization to maintain peace based on justice, all our plans will have to be worked out through practice rather than through a prepared "blueprint." One of the criticisms that may, in justice, be leveled against the League of Nations is that it was something new, made on the pattern of a perfect world organization and put before a world of nations that had had no experience in working under such terms or circumstances. If we do the work that needs to be done by following the method of "trial and error," we can build a new world order that will be strong enough to guarantee real security from fear and from want.

Ultimately, an international conference will have to be held to agree upon and establish the permanent form and machinery of the new "League of Nations"—by whatever name it may be called. The United Nations probably will set up a board of strategy with authority to appoint commissions to study such questions as economics, world trade, immigration, the resettlement of uprooted populations, the future of colonies not yet able to care for themselves, questions relating to collective security—such as building up a permanent international police force to maintain law and order among the nations—and hundreds of other problems that will have to be settled. If the peace conference is thus planned and if the nations, through their representatives, have worked together in the commissions over a long enough period, then when the delegates meet there will be more facts and fewer hates, more determination to find a way out, and less of a desire for revenge. This is, indeed, a huge undertaking; but it can be done.

In developing these plans it will become evident that there are a large number of international agencies that have held over from the interim period between World War I and the outbreak of this war, such as the World Court, the International Labor Office, the Commission on Intellectual Co-operation, as well as other facilities that have been established at The Hague and Geneva by the League of Nations. All these agencies will be available and will be of infinite value in guiding those who will be responsible for carrying out the plans of rebuilding the world.

No international organization will be effective unless it has behind it an adequate armed police force. The technicalities involved in providing such a force and the methods of making it effective are so intricate that this question will require a great deal of careful study. The airplane and other modern weapons and methods of making war add to the difficulties; but these advances make it even more necessary that the force required to maintain peace shall be used with the greatest care and precision, for it must be clear that force in and of itself is never wholly effective.

Mr. Elmer Davis said some months ago: "It will take much wisdom, much co-operative effort, and much surrender of private, short-sighted, and sectional self-interest, to make these things come true. But the goal is freedom from want—individual security and national prosperity—and is everlastingly worth striving for."

In conclusion, we all know that war is the outgrowth of the anarchy throughout the world in the relations of the nations with each other. There can be no peace unless it is organized on a world-wide basis, with each nation giving up part of its rights and privileges for the greater economic and political security to be found within the community of nations. This community must be provided with a police force, courts, parliaments, and such other instruments as will guarantee security for each nation on the principle of "all for one and one for all." Behind such an exercise of power there must be the good will and moral support of all the citizens of each nation. Religion can and ought to supply this spiritual backing. One of our American delegates at the League of Nations Disarmament Conference in 1932, speaking of the deadlock, said in effect that every man in the conference knew what he *ought* to do to get rid of the arms being piled up and, further, that every man knew that, unless something could stop the enormous increase, it would lead to the most terrible war in all history. Yet knowing these facts, he said: "Not one delegate here dares to take the lead in proposing a simple plan for the reduction and limitation of armaments, because he knows that his government will not support such a course and that the folks back home have not the moral fortitude to stand behind the government even if it permitted its delegates to make such a proposal."

How can we create the proper moral atmosphere so that the international agreements can be carried out and the machinery of the world community operate effectively? This is the paramount issue to which we must all give our thought and attention.

SOVIET RUSSIA AND THE POSTWAR WORLD

JOHN L. CHILDS

Professor of the Philosophy of Education
Teachers College, Columbia University

FOR OVER A QUARTER OF A CENTURY SOVIET RUSSIA HAS BEEN the subject of a sharp and world-wide controversy. On one side there have been the ardent defenders who have found nothing but good in the results of the Revolution, and who have contended that the new pattern of the economy and government of the Soviet Union constitutes the true and historically determined pattern of democratic and industrial society. Opposed to them have been the hostile critics who have regarded the Revolutionary system as contrary to the laws of God and of nature, who have rejoiced in Soviet Russia's difficulties and inner conflicts, and who have repeatedly predicted and earnestly longed for her early collapse. As the years have passed, many have moved from one to the other side of this controversy. Early admirers have turned into disillusioned and bitter critics; former opponents have changed into warm supporters.

Even as distinguished and informed a leader as Winston Churchill has had difficulty in making up his mind about the Soviet Union. In one of his speeches, for example, he described her as: "A riddle wrapped in a mystery inside an enigma."

But at the critical time of the invasion of Finland he found no difficulty in solving the "mystery" of Soviet Russia and exposing her real nature to the world. He then declared:

The service rendered by Finland to mankind is magnificent. They have exposed, for all the world to see, the military in-

138

capacity of the Red Army and of the Red Air Force. Many illusions about Soviet Russia have been dispelled in these few fierce weeks of fighting in the Arctic Circle. Everyone can see how Communism rots the soul of a nation; how it makes that nation abject and hungry in peace, and proves it base and abominable in war.

But clear and definite as this summary of Russian Communism is, it failed to settle the problem of the Soviet Union in the mind of Winston Churchill. Having witnessed and gained much from the more recent heroic deeds of the leaders, the armed forces, and the valiant people of Soviet Russia, the Prime Minister of Britain once again reviewed and reversed his estimate of her national significance and power. In a speech given at the London Lord Mayor's luncheon in November, 1943, he declared:

I gladly admit, and indeed proclaim, that the outstanding event of this famous year has been the victorious advance of the Russian armies from the Volga westward. . . .

In this process the Russian Soviet armies have inflicted deep and dire injury upon the whole life structure of the German military power. That monstrous juggernaut engine of German might and tyranny has been beaten . . . to an extent which may well prove mortal.

We and our American allies have done and are doing our best to bring our forces across the seas and oceans into action against the enemy. And I rate the Anglo-American air attack on Germany as one of the prime forces of the impending ruin of the Hitlerite regime.

But it must never be forgotten that there was nothing in the whole world, nor could there have been created for several years, any military organism which could either have given the blows which Russia has given or survive the losses which Russia has borne.

Whether this will be the final verdict of Winston Churchill on the strength and worth of the Soviet Union, I do not venture to predict. It is already abundantly clear, however, that the magnificent part Russia has played in the struggle against Fascism has not closed the controversy about her.[1] The conflict of the political sects about the nature, the morality, the industrial efficiency, the social and political democracy, and the ultimate destiny of the Soviet Union continues as before. We still have those who insist that Soviet Russia is merely a totalitarian, military dictatorship, and that from the standpoint of democracy there is little, if anything, to choose between the Communism of Stalin and the Nazism of Hitler. Events will ultimately show, it is held, that it is as impossible to do business with the one as with the other. We also have those who are now more convinced than ever that the Soviet Union is the sole hope of the world, the supreme fulfillment of the age-long aspiration of the human race for equality, justice, freedom, and democratic brotherhood.

Most of the people of the world, however, have never accepted either of these extreme positions. They have preferred to suspend judgment and to let the Soviet Union carry on its bold experiment. They have not wanted foreign influences—either friendly or hostile—to determine the ultimate fate of this Russian socialist undertaking. Hence, they have felt that the people of the Soviet Union should enjoy freedom to work out their own internal arrangements in economy and government. Similarly, they have opposed the efforts of the Russian revolutionists to project themselves into the domestic affairs of other countries. Today, as a result of the experiences of the war, the common people of the United Nations have developed two convictions about Soviet Russia which will necessarily condition the pattern of approach to the tasks of the postwar world.

The first of these is the conviction that the Soviet Union has played a decisive role in the defeat of the Fascist menace. This conviction is particularly strong among the working people of the world, who for very cogent reasons have been

---

[1] The term "Fascism" is used in this chapter to denote *all* of the totalitarian states of the Axis, not merely the regime of Mussolini in Italy.

much less pacifist in this than in the first World War. Slowly but surely the ruthless behavior of Germany, Italy, and Japan bred in the minds of the working people the conclusion that this brand of aggression had to be stopped, and that the common man had a real stake in a war undertaken to eliminate this Fascist menace. Even in the United States there has been much less talk about this war's being merely another imperialist struggle for power in which we as a nation have no vital interest at stake. We now perceive that our policy of neutrality of the 'thirties—a policy which assumed that the distinction between the Fascist Powers of aggresion and their national victims was of no moment to us—was an illusion and a very dangerous evasion of a national responsibility.

We also are now aware that, following the collapse of France, the Axis Powers had a real chance to win this war and to become dominant in Europe, Asia, and Africa. Had the Fascist totalitarian forces achieved this dominance in the rest of the world, it is conceivable that the Western Hemisphere could have retained its independence, but clearly only at the cost of transforming itself into an armed fortress under the industrial and military aegis of the United States. Despite the crushing internal and external burdens this would have put upon our nation, we might still have preserved some of the essentials of the American way of life; but it is evident that many of the values which we have cherished under the name of democracy would not have long survived in such a frankly military regime.

As Winston Churchill now admits, the part Soviet Russia has played in removing this menace through the destruction of the Fascist forces is primary. It is because of the sacrifice and heroic resistance of her people and armies that the prospect of the total defeat of the Hitler forces is now assured. The common people of the United Nations, including those of our own country, are keenly aware of the importance of this contribution of the Soviet Union to the common struggle; and their general recognition of the debt we owe Russia

141

is a political fact of the greatest importance. No thinking about the organization of the postwar world can be soundly based which does not take it into account. The plain fact is that without the indispensable contribution of the Soviet Union the other members of the United Nations probably would never have won the right to undertake the organization of the postwar world. The central importance of this conviction in the mind of the ordinary citizen is in no way lessened by recognition of the equally significant fact that without the help of Britain and America the Soviet Union also would probably have been defeated.

The second of these deep-lying convictions of the common man is that the Soviet Union has demonstrated that she is one of the really great powers, and that no plan for the organization of the postwar world which seeks to remove the threat of aggressive war can possibly succeed unles it includes her as a full partner. Even liberals, and democratic internationalists, who have been slow to develop an adequate theory of the role of power in the affairs of mankind, now realize that the co-operation of the Soviet Union is a condition essential to the stable organization of the postwar world.

This vast strength of the Soviet Union derives from many and various factors.

First is the fact of her immense territory. The size of the Soviet Union is almost three times that of the United States, and more than forty times that of France. This vast region has a range of climate from subtropical in the south to arctic temperatures along the extended northern border. It provides rich wheat and cotton lands, vast cattle ranges, excellent dairy regions, and produces in abundance a wide variety of fruits and vegetables.

Second is the fact of her rich resourecs in minerals, oils, forests and water power. According to Soviet estimates, the U.S.S.R. "contains 55 per cent of the world's oil, 28 per cent of the world's power capacity, 21 per cent of the iron, one-third of the forest reserves. It is second to Canada in its

142

supplies of nickel and possesses large stores of manganese, asbestos, zinc, lead, copper, and bauxite. It is the second largest gold producer in the world."

Third is the fact of her large and rapidly growing population. She is now inhabited by close to two hundred million people, and some predict that within a generation her population will approach three hundred millions. Her peoples are of many different races and nationalities, and the Soviet Union has been unusually successful in comprehending these different cultural groups within a common national authority. All observers remark on the depth of the patriotism of the Russian people, and the extent to which national feeling and loyalty have been aroused by the bitter struggle with Hitler's invading hordes. Pride in the past and deep hope for the future are characteristics of this vast and sturdy people to whom the resources of education, science, and culture are at last being made available. The illiterate peasant, steeped in superstition, is rapidly being supplanted by the literate and technically trained worker of factory and farm.

Fourth is the fact of her strategic location. As one observer has remarked: "Russia is neither Europe nor Asia. She is a world by herself, situated between Europe and Asia, and, in a way, belonging to both."

Another close student of the Soviet Union and the Far East has recently written:

It is hard for the imagination to grasp the increase of relative strength which the Soviet Union will experience if and when Germany and Japan are completely knocked out and reduced to impotence as military powers. Given this condition, Stalin will possess far and away the greatest combination of military and industrial strength between the Atlantic and the Pacific. It will be of momentous consequence for the future of the world how he uses this strength.

Not only do Soviet Russia's huge population, rich resources, and geographical position combine to make her the supreme

143

land power of our interdependent world, but also she is so situated that she is bound to exert great control over the future development of those world airways which will connect not only Europe with Asia but the hemispheres of the East and the West.

Fifth is the fact of her wholehearted commitment to the use of the resources of science and technology for the increase of production. Great as have been her losses in the war, it is certain that her industrial strength has by no means been destroyed, and, once hostilities end, we may anticipate that she will experience an unprecedented industrial recovery and further development. Indeed, the United States and the Soviet Union are the only countries of the whole world which include within their own borders that combination of agricultural and industrial materials which make possible the development of anything approximating a self-sufficient economy. The Soviet Union, stimulated by the experiences of this great war, may be expected to organize for production at a greatly accelerated rate once her territory is freed from the enemy forces. Her nationalized economy, controlled as it is by unified planning agencies, is almost ideally designed to undertake a national program of agricultural and industrial rehabilitation and expansion, a program in which the major goals are easily defined and popularly approved.

Sixth is the fact of her great prestige among the colored, exploited, and underprivileged peoples of the world. That the Soviet Union now enjoys a certain strength because of this popular response of groups in other countries cannot be doubted. Part of this strength derives from the sympathy given her by elements in the populations of the Western capitalist democracies who suffer from insecurity, unemployment, and want, and who resent the failure of their own national systems of economy and government to make available to them that enriched mode of life now made possible by the discoveries and inventions of science and technology. An even greater fund of approval is found among the vast populations of the colored and colonial peoples who feel that they have been exploited economically, politically, and culturally by an imperialist system designed to serve the interests of the Westerner and to perpetuate his position of dominance. These groups, to be sure, may not like all of the current practices of the Soviet Union; but they, nevertheless, are happy to know that an alternative exists to that system under which they life. The presence of these underprivileged and discontented groups in the West and the East who look with hope to the Soviet Union as a possible source of liberation, has played an important role in the affairs of the world during the past twenty-five years. It has certainly contributed to the present prestige of the first socialist state in the international field.

But today not merely the common people but the heads of governments also are convinced of the economic, military, and political strength of Soviet Russia. For a considerable period, at least, after the surrender of the Axis Powers, Moscow will be one of the foremost centers of influence in the world. Although the war is still in process, we have already held one of the most far-reaching conferences on the postwar world which will be organized. It is significant that this conference was held not in Washington, not in London, but in Moscow. In his report to the House of Commons on the results of this tripartite conference, Anthony Eden did not exaggerate when he said:

The truth must be faced that it is on the part of these three powers principally that will lie the responsibility for insuring that this war be followed by lasting peace. If they could agree together there is no point that is not capable of final solution. If they do not agree together there is no international event which could not become an international problem.

What, then, is the prospect that these three world powers can collaborate in the postwar tasks, and that their collaboration will be of a character which will make for world security

145

and peace? Let it be said at once that the outlook for this kind of co-operation is much more promising today than it was before the Moscow Conference was held, even though it is clear from the official report of the gathering that many basic problems remain to be resolved. According to the Joint Communiqué:

The agendas included all questions submitted for discussion by the three Governments. Some of the questions called for final decisions, and these were taken. On other questions, after discussion, decisions of principle were taken. . . . Other questions again were disposed of by an exchange of views.

Before a complete judgment of the Moscow Conference can be made, we shall have to know just what were the questions which in the words of the Joint Communiqué "were disposed of by an exchange of views." It is apparent, this really means, in more straightforward language, that consideration of certain difficult problems was postponed because the various participants held views which were in too deep conflict to be adjusted or compromised at this first conference. But to say that not everything was accomplished at the Moscow gathering is not to say that the conference was not a substantial success.

William H. Chamberlain, author of *The Russian Enigma* and a close student of international affairs, heads a recent article on the conference in *The New Leader* with the question, "Was Moscow an Eastern-European Munich?" He grants the basic importance of some of the decisions taken at the Moscow meeting, but he fears that they may have been accompanied by an agreement on the part of Britain and the United States to let the Soviet Union have its own way on the question of the Baltic States and Poland. A capitulation of this sort "to Stalin's territorial demands," he believes, would vitiate "in advance by obvious injustice" the proposal for a world organization. Mr. Chamberlain does not assert that we have thus capitulated to Stalin's demands, but he considers that "the silences of Moscow are ominous and disquieting."

The Administrative Board of the National Catholic Welfare Conference also voices this fear. It says:

The Declarations of the Moscow Conference do, indeed, open the way to necessary international co-operation for peace as well as for war. In this they represent a definite step in the right direction. They do not, however, dispel the fear that compromises on the ideals of the Atlantic Charter are in prospect. Some things these documents imply by statement and more significantly still by omission leave an uneasiness in the minds intent on peace with justice to all.

The New Republic, on the other hand, in its interpretaion of the significance of the conference declares:

It is no exaggeration to say that, despite all the difficulties that still lie ahead, last week's actions by the Moscow Conference and by the [U. S.] Senate have swung open the portals on a new world.

My own estimate of the achievements of the conference is, on the whole, closer to that of the *New Republic* than it is to that of Mr. Chamberlain and the Catholic Welfare Conference. Clearly many difficult problems remain. The promise of Moscow may never be fulfilled, for the task of organizing the world for security, peace, and material and cultural advance is a huge task—events may show that it is still a task beyond the present powers of the human race. But those who hold that such an organization of the world constitutes a necessary and a possible present program find much in the beginning made at Moscow to give them encouragement.

In the first place, it is clear that at this conference the Soviet Union, Britain, and the United States finally achieved important understandings about the present critical military task. These understandings about the management of the common struggle with the Fascist forces are crucial, because

147

we should remember that the defeat of these forces is a necessary precondition to the organization of the world for security and peace. As a result of the conference, it is now agreed that hostilities are to be continued until the Axis Powers "have laid down their arms on the basis of unconditional surrender." Thus the Joint Four-Nation Declaration cuts the ground from under any hope that Hitler may have entertained that he could avoid defeat by a policy of "divide and conquer."

In the second place, the conference makes it clear that these powers are now united in the understanding that the primary objective of the war is the defeat and destruction of the pattern and the forces of Fascism. The united policy regarding Italy, the three powers state, is "based upon the fundamental principle that Fascism and all its evil influence and configuration shall be completely destroyed and that the Italian people shall be given every opportunity to establish governmental and other institutions based upon democratic principles." Clearly, it is also assumed that this basic principle is to govern future dealings of the United Nations not only with the Italian situation but with the whole European situation. This apparently means that the mistaken effort to restore reactionary and semi-Fascist governments in Europe is to be abandoned in favor of positive support of liberal and democratic groups.

In the third place, the conference provides machinery for the continuation of the collaboration of the principal powers among the United Nations. This collaboration is to begin at once. It is to deal with military, economic, and political questions. It is to continue not only for the period of the war but also into the period following the end of hostilities. It is also recognized that this co-operation and collaboration must be exercised in the spirit of a trusteeship for all the peace-loving nations.

Concrete means for attaining this collaboration on general European matters is provided in the plan for a European

148

Advisory Commission, composed of representatives of these three governments, which is to have headquarters in London. An Advisory Council on Italy was also established; and this provides, in addition to those of the three powers, for representatives of the French Committee of National Liberation and, in time, of Greece and Yugoslavia.

On broader problems of the postwar world and the establishment of a general international organization, four powers—America, Britain, China, and Soviet Russia—agree to "consult with one another and as occasion requires with other members of the United Nations with a view to joint action on behalf of the community of nations."

Of supreme importance is the pledge of these four powers to the effect "that after the termination of hostilities they will not employ their military forces within the territories of other States except for the purposes envisaged in this declaration and after joint consultation."

As one who has contended for some time that the possibility of peace depended upon the possibility of understanding and co-operation on the part of these four powers, I consider the foregoing agreements of fundamental importance. They mean that, inspite of important differences in economic and political systems, these great nations have concluded after due deliberation that their interests, and the interests of the peoples of the world for whom they act as trustees, will be better served if they collaborate than if they continue to work isolated from one another.

Thus the Moscow Conference has built two bridges. One is the bridge between the world of the capitalist democracies and the world of Communism. The other is the bridge between the world of the white man of the West and the colored peoples of the East. Everything depends upon whether these two bridges continue to stand. Time alone will give the answer. But at least we can be grateful that the Moscow Conference has succeeded in providing these indispensable means of communication, consultation, and collaboration.

149

In the fourth place, and finally, the conference at Moscow definitely envisages more than a mere power alliance of victors. The Four-Nation Declaration recognizes that, in our interdependent world, aggressive war is an offense against the human race. It proposes an organization of the world to get rid of this menace. The four powers promise to establish "at the earliest practicable date a general international organization, based on the principle of the sovereign equality of all peace-loving States, and open to membership by all such States, large and small, for the maintenance of international peace and security." They also agree "that they will confer and co-operate with one another and with other members of the United Nations to bring about a practicable general agreement with respect to the regulation of armaments in the postwar period."

Here, again, time will disclose the value of these promises. They may, of course, degenerate into mere empty phrases. Or they may serve as the governing principles of a determined movement to develop a stable and just system of mutual security which will make possible progressive reductions in the heavy burden of national armaments. But, regardless of what the eventual outcome may be, the conference at Moscow has done important preliminary work in defining the principles of a democratic world order and in developing concrete machinery by which the co-operative task of its organization can be undertaken. Indeed, the achievements of Moscow seem to be more substantial than most dared to hope. This is particularly true if Anthony Eden accurately described the atmosphere of the conference when he said to the House of Commons: "As we worked, the sense of confidence grew. This, in turn, seemed to give added momentum to our progress so that it was better in the middle than in the beginning, and better again at the end than in the middle."

One of the significant features of this momentous gathering on world affairs is the subordinate part the nations of Western Europe played in it. This has both its negative and positive

150

aspects. Ultimately these nations, taken as a unit, will have to play an important part in the shaping of postwar affairs. The world cannot be organized for lasting peace without their co-operation. On the other hand, it is equally important for all to recognize that Europe is not the world, and that the center of political gravity no longer resides in Western Europe. Indeed, the sooner the nations of Western Europe realize that their day of world domination is past, the better the prospect of creating a genuine international organization. China, Soviet Russia, Great Britain, and the United States constitute much more representative, powerful, and stable bases for a world organization than could be found in any possible combination of these European nations.

If these Great Powers can continue to collaborate, there is a possibility that the world may be organized for a lasting peace. Without their collaboration the possibility of a system of mutual security is slight indeed. The Pact of Moscow strengthens the possibility of that co-operation; and it also promises the organization of a democratic international authority which, in time, is to supersede the four-power arrangement. To be sure, if the promise of the Moscow Conference is actually to be fulfilled, many adjustments and concessions will have to be made. Some of the most important of these national accommodations are already in process.

On her side, Soviet Russia has moved to give up her policy of isolation. The decisions taken at Moscow imply that she is disposed to participate in a program of international co-operation. It is to be hoped that her territorial demands will be in harmony with this democratic and peaceful international aim. Great as is her present prestige, it could be dissipated were she to launch upon an imperialist program of expansion and exploitation.

The Soviet Union has also given some evidence that she recognizes that there is a contradiction between sharing in a program of international co-operation designed to develop a world organization and, at the same time, giving her support

151

to a political instrumentality which is designed to disrupt and overthrow the systems of economy and government now established in the other countries of the United Nations. As a result, she has officially repudiated the historic policy of the Third International and has announced that communist parties in the various countries of the world should henceforth operate as autonomous bodies. Unfortunately, these parties have, as yet, given no important evidence that they intend to take this more dignified role. Judged by their present concrete deeds, these communist national movements seem to carry on much as before. One striking illustration of this is their unanimous and enthusiastic endorsement of the proposal from Moscow that their hitherto much prized International be dissolved. So far as my knowledge goes, not a single one of these national communist parties entered any protest to this action. Similarly, they continue to act in all other matters as they imagine the interests and the rulers of the Soviet Union demand. For the present, this means all-out participation in the nation's war effort even at times at the expense of hard-won social and labor gains. Of course, all of this may be purely coincidental. The acid test will come when the problems of postwar reconstruction are undertaken. Then we shall soon discover whether these several national communist parties now really stand on their own foundations, and advocate policies which they themselves have formulated in response to the conditions of their own countries, or whether they are still cast in the role of fifth columnists—the obedient agents of a foreign power.

Finally, much will depend, so far as the Soviet Union is concerned, on the future of her dictatorship. It may be hoped that, as a result of the great unity achieved in the defense of the fatherland, the present ruling class will have less to fear from dissident groups, and hence will be inclined to put into operation its deferred plans for developing more democratic participation and control in the actual processes by which governmental policies are made. It may also be hoped that the experiences of the war, the rising standard of living, and the spread of education will make the rank and file of the population more insistent in its demand for greater democratization of the Soviet state.

World public opinion will undoubtedly play a part in all of this. The dissolution of the Communist International and the relaxation of the restrictions on religion indicate that the rulers of Soviet Russia are not indifferent to the views of the outside world.

More fundamental, however, will be the actual trend of events in the international sphere. One of the sources of strength of the dictatorship has been the feeling of the Russians that they were ringed by hostile, imperialistic nations who were longing for the chance to destroy their socialist state. The need of defense against an external foe was a powerful factor in prompting the people of the Soviet Union to submit to a highly centralized form of government. Should postwar developments demonstrate that there is no sound basis for this fear of attack from without, and should the leaders of the Soviet Union continue to work along the democratic and international lines defined in the Four-Power Pact, there is reason to hope that the internal dictatorship will be progressively modified. It is very difficult for a nation to co-operate in a many-sided international program and at the same time keep its people ignorant of the ways of life and the institutions of other nations.

But Soviet Russia is not the only nation which will have to make concessions and readjustments if a genuine system of collective security is to be developed. The United Kingdom and the United States also have to undertake certain reconstructions in their traditional outlooks and practices. Fortunately, here also some of the needed readjustments are already in process.

One of these is the decision of the United States to abandon its historic policy of isolation. This decision is officially involved in the Moscow commitments, and the most basic of all of these has fortunately already been incorporated into the text of the resolution adopted by an overwhelming vote by the United States Senate. Highly impressive also are the specific instrumentalities we are organizing and sharing in, such as the United Nations Relief and Rehabilitation Administration; Lend-Lease; the Conference on Food and Agriculture; the International Labor Office; and other agencies for international co-operation in the fields of public health, currency, education, and the like. Many things will become more possible in other countries if we remain firm in this determination to use our great material, economic, political, and moral strength to help develop a world community. Our wholehearted participation may mark the difference between success and failure in this international enterprise.

A second adjustment on the part of both Britain and the United States is inherent in the resolve to treat Soviet Russia very differently from the way we treated her at the close of the first World War. We should not forget that at that time we "co-operated," for a period, even to the extent of the use of our armed forces, with the White Russian counter-revolutionary factions which were seeking to overthrow the Soviet government. Nor should we forget that for a considerable period the Soviet Union was not admitted to the League of Nations, that even after she was admitted she was treated with scant regard, and that it was sixteen years after the establishment of the new Russian state before its government was formally recognized by the United States.

If the Moscow Pact means anything, it means that both Britain and the United States are now pledged to abandon all further thought of isolating or surrounding the Soviet Union with a belt of hostile buffer states. But the agreements made at Moscow have their positive as well as their negative implications. They clearly imply that we are now ready to meet the Soviet Union half way, and that we hope to work side by side with her in the varied tasks of the postwar world. This means, as I have already emphasized, that we must cease trying to restore broken-down monarchies and semi-fascist classes and groups to places of power in postwar Europe, and must stand ready instead, as the Agreement on Italy specifically states, to use our influence to strengthen the forces which are seeking to build a new and more democratic Europe.

Finally, the Moscow Pact should also bring to an end further talk about an Anglo-American alliance. Such a restricted alliance would hinder, not help, us to build a lasting, democratic organization of the world. It would strengthen the hope of the reactionary groups in both our country and Britain that they need not continue with the kind of reorganization of domestic institutions required to maintain production, full employment, and social security. It would also have a tragic effect on the peoples of the East; for, regardless of our protestations, they would interpret it to mean that the old program of imperialistic domination and exploitation was to be perpetuated. Finally, it would not harmonize with our avowed purpose to co-operate with Soviet Russia as a full and equal partner. Alliances may start as innocent plans for promoting democratic and universal ends, but they generally finish by advancing the interests of limited groups, and they also easily become instrumentalities which are aimed at other nations. If we mean to work on the basis of the principles so excellently defined in the four-power Moscow agreement, we have no need for limited and exclusive alliance. Such an Anglo-American alliance would be apt to call into being another alliance of powers to offset it, and that would mean we were back once again at the old game of power politics with all that implies.

In conclusion, I would like to say a word about the future relations of the Soviet Union and our own country. At the close of the war and for a considerable period thereafter, these two great continental nations will be the two most powerful states in the world. If we grow in understanding and co-operation, the world can have peace. If we let our differences in ideology, in economy, and in government breed suspicion, hostility, and antagonism, the present global struggle will almost surely be followed by another and more terrible war.

Undoubtedly each of these two great continental powers would like to see certain important changes take place in the doctrines and institutions of the other. The Soviet Union, on her side, would like to see the United States transformed into a completely socialist society from which all racial and class privileges are eliminated. The United States, on her side, would like to see the Soviet Union move rapidly to abolish the dictatorship and establish a complete system of civil liberties and political, intellectual, and religious freedoms. Regardless of how desirable these changes might be from either standpoint, I do not believe that they should be made a condition of sincere collaboration. Neither do I believe that international co-operation can wait until all desirable improvements have been made within the internal affairs of these two nations. If we are to succeed in laying the foundations for a new civilization, we must recognize the principle of cultural pluralism. There is no way by which either the Soviet Union or the United States can impose its patterns of life upon the other. To attempt this is to fail to respond to the opportunities and the imperatives of the age.

I gather a similar conclusion and compulsion must have been in the minds of the American and Russian leaders who met at Moscow. Let us hope that the superb work there started by our leaders will be backed by such a tide of public opinion in both countries that the conference of Moscow will stand in history as the occasion when the portals began to open to a new and better day in the affairs of mankind.

ECONOMIC WELFARE AND WORLD PEACE

H. Gordon Hayes

Professor of Economics, Ohio State University

I

IT IS WELL TO CONNECT THE TWO TERMS "ECONOMIC WELFARE" and "world peace." Our hearts turn toward the possibility of an early peace and a long-enduring one. It seems to me that it is possible that no one who is now living will see another major war. But a hundred years of peace will not come merely because men and women of good will wish it to come. No group of people ever desired more firmly that peace should continue forever than did the people of America, England, France, and Russia in the years from the close of the first World War to the eve of the breaking out of this one. Further, large groups of Germans and Japanese—there were many such in each of these two countries—just as fervently desired peace as did any of us.

But we in this country were betrayed by our political leaders, as Wendell Willkie sets forth in the closing chapter of his book, *One World*. We abandoned the League, which the hopes and dreams of men, largely of this country, had created. It is possible that the American people may be sold down the river again, although it does not appear very probable that that will happen. For we shall, it appears now, be on the alert. Certainly we must be watchful and purposeful and resourceful if we are to fulfill the great vision of Isaiah which has been so long deferred.

Not only must we see to it that we as a nation play our rightful part in keeping the peace of the world; we must also see to it that our economic arrangements promote peace

157

and not discord among the peoples of the world. This brings me to my topic—economic welfare and world peace. First, let me emphasize that I by no means hold the view that wars are to be explained by—or are caused by—economic factors alone. Economists as I have met them and read from them do not accept the economic interpretation of human behavior in this crude form. Such ideas prevail only among noneconomists, or, I should say, among non-social scientists.

II

Certainly wars have many causes. And there is one that is very important—perhaps the cause of more wars than any other, or of all other causes put together—which is not economic at all, although economic matters are often used as supplemental to or even as a front to this basic force. I refer to the desire for glory—the desire to be a big man, to be a big group of men, to be a glorious nation. This comes out of what John Maynard Keynes has well called, in reference to business enterprise, animal spirits. Animal spirits—muscular energy, the desire to do something, the desire to track down something. We all have some of this. We couldn't make a living without it. We couldn't build churches without it— nor schools and colleges. We couldn't get husbands or wives without it. Nor make speeches. How strange that we pay so little attention to this factor in relation to he causes of war. William James did, you recall. It was because of such considerations that he proposed a *moral equivalent to war*.

Plutarch has a delightful tale about the Greek warrior Pyrrhus, of approximately 300 B.C., that illustrates this point. Pyrrhus had retired to his kingdom of Epirus, after conquering Macedonia; and, says Plutarch, he had a fair occasion given him by fortune to enjoy himself in quiet and to govern his kingdom in peace. But his nature was such that life was insufferable if he was not annoying others or being annoyed by them. So he relieved his energy by fitting out an expedition against Rome. There was at his court a Thessalonian named Cineas, and he asked Pyrrhus what he would do next if it pleased heaven that he should conquer the Romans.

"Why," said Pyrrhus, "there will not then be any tribe in all Italy, whether Greek or barbarian, that we shall not be able to overcome."

"And what then?" asked Cineas.

"Why," said Pyrrhus, "there lies Sicily with her arms open to receive us."

"And what next when you have taken Sicily?"

"Why," said Pyrrhus, "there are Carthage and Lybia just across the water that we shall take."

"And when you have conquered them all, what then?"

"Then," said Pyrrhus, "we shall take our ease and drink and be merry."

And Cineas, having brought him this far, says Plutarch, replied: "What hinders us from doing that now since we already have in our hands those things which you propose to arrive at through seas of blood and toil and danger which we must both cause and suffer?"

This discourse, adds Plutarch, caused Pyrrhus much pain but produced no reformation.

He went on to his battles, I may add, but won his battles with the Romans at such cost that the term "Pyrrhic victory" is part of our language. A modern Pyrrhus would talk about his nation's being a have-not nation, about needing colonies and raw materials, about raising the scale of living at home by enlarging the nation's territory. He would talk in this way because the world now looks askance at the military marauder and requires justification in terms of economic welfare.

III

Of course, this have-not matter is largely nonsense as a cause of war. Switzerland is certainly a have-not nation if there is one anywhere, but she gets along without conquest. Similarly, any small nation is almost necessarily limited in its resources. It gets on as do the people of Delaware and

Columbus, by swapping goods and services that they produce for the goods and services that other regions produce. During all the talk about have-not nations in the 1920's and 1930's, I was always brought back to the simple point that there wasn't a thing that the Germans and Japanese claimed to need that we in this country wouldn't sell them. Cotton, iron, foodstuffs—we were certainly willing to sell anything that we had except the Washington Monument and the Statue of Liberty. We stood ready to sell on easy terms, too. We preferred, indeed, to sell our goods for gold which we could bury or for pieces of paper which would be a long time coming due. But men with the lust for blood beat themselves on the chest and talked of having to conquer in order to eat. What the Germans needed with their refined skills in making luxury goods of all sorts was markets in London, Paris, New York. There was nothing to be gained on this score by taking Austria with its impoverished peasant population, nor Czechoslovakia, nor Poland. The real reason for wanting these territories and these peoples was something quite other than economic.

You are all familiar, I am sure, with data in respect to Germany's colonies before the first World War. The imports into Germany from her colonies in 1912 and 1913 amounted to only 0.5 per cent of all German imports, and her exports to her colonies for these two years amounted to only 0.6 per cent of all her exports. For the twenty years before the war, Germany's trade with her colonies amounted to only 0.5 per cent of her total foreign trade. The colonial trade of the world in 1936 is estimated to have amounted to less than 10 per cent of the total imports and exports of all the nations in the world.

It is often insisted that nations need to carry on successive wars of conquest in order to have territory into which their surplus populations may migrate. Here again references to the data show that the position taken is unsound. In July, 1914, for example, there were only 24,000 Germans, including soldiers and police, in all the German colonies. Many Japanese died in the war against Russia, which resulted in the Japanese' having an opportunity to migrate to Manchuria; but during the next twenty-five years fewer Japanese migrated to Manchuria than died in the war to make this possible.

But while an urge to fight, to conquer, to achieve glory, is an important factor in inciting nations to military aggression, there are also primitive economic considerations that promote conflict. Man does not live by bread alone, but he cannot live without it. And within reasonable limits he can live a more wholesome life as his basic economic needs are satisfied. Hence nations may be impelled to war in the hope of improving their economic position. Furthermore, economic distress furnishes a basis for the development of a war spirit by men whose major interests are those of Pyrrhus. Let us now turn to a consideration of the economic factors that disturb the peace of the world.

IV

Capitalist nations are, and since the advent of capitalism have been, interested in having markets for exports. Indeed, there has been a big struggle for net exports. Each capitalist nation has wanted to sell, but it has not wished to buy. We find statements to this effect throughout our history. A great deal was said along this line at the time of the Spanish American War. Senator Beveridge of Indiana, for example, in a lecture entitled "The March of the Flag," which he gave in all parts of the country, said that we had more workers than jobs, that we had more capacity than output, that we were able to produce more than we were able to consume. This came, he said, because of a lack of markets. The islands which we had acquired, Beveridge insisted, would furnish us an opportunity to sell such a large quantity of goods that we would be able to put every mill in operation and set all of our spindles humming. There was nothing here of our getting anything for these exports except a chance to work.

161

We were to sell—not buy. Mr. Hoover talked to this same effect while a candidate for the presidency. And today we are taking great delight in the fact that the other nations of the world will wish to buy from us extensively when the war is over. This quest for net exports has undoubtedly been a factor throughout the years in leading nations to war. Nations have wished to defend the opportunities to sell that they had already acquired and to secure new opportunities as a result of additional conquests.

Another factor making for war, that is closely related to this, is that when net exports have resulted in the making of investments in a foreign country, it then has often become the policy of the home government to protect these investments. Mr. Will Rogers called attention to this matter in an interesting fashion some twenty years ago. He said that the Chinese were wanting to have a civil war and that the British and Americans were interfering with their plans. When we wanted to have a civil war, asked Rogers, what did the Chinese do? Did they send their gunboats up the Mississippi River to protect their laundries at Memphis? No, said Rogers, the Chinese government sent out word that each Chink must look after his own washboard. But other nations send their gunboats, and this fans the flames of war.

Another relation between economic factors and war is found in the simple fact that the making and selling of war goods is a very profitable business and that capitalists have not been above accepting this kind of trade. Indeed, as everybody knows, a great deal of attention has been given by the so-called merchants of death to the fomenting of war scares in order to increase the sale of armaments.

V

Aside from the matter of businessmen's making money out of war and preparations for war, one must not overlook the point that millions of persons have had employment in producing war goods who might otherwise have been out of

162

work. The very fact of insecurity under capitalism must be held to be a factor that promotes war. Indeed, economic insecurity is perhaps the most significant of all the economic factors that make for war. Certainly, economic life under capitalism is not secure. And, paradoxically as it may seem, the better we do under capitalism, the more we contribute to our general insecurity. If we all come to have a high standard of living, it becomes more easily possible for us to withhold purchases and thereby induce unemployment than if we lived generally on a relatively low scale. Similarly, the more durable we make our goods, the easier it is for us to postpone replacing them and thus interrupt sales and induce unemployment.

Unemployment as we know it today is unquestionably one of the greatest scourges to which the human race has been subject. The degradation of personality which it induces makes its ravages comparable to that of the devastating plagues of the past. Nothing is perhaps worse than for individuals to come to feel that there is no function they can perform in the society of which they are members. The attitudes which are thereby generated make the unemployed easy victims for anyone who promises them a function. It was out of unemployment in Italy and Germany that Mussolini and Hitler rose to power. As one writer said of the Italians, the young men had nothing to lose but their boredom.

We need to note especially that unemployment in the United States is particularly bad in so far as the rest of the world is concerned. Unemployment here is easily communicated to the people of other countries. During the years 1925-29 the people of the United States imported more than four billion dollars of goods every year. But during the years 1932-34 our average imports amounted to less than one and a half billion dollars per year. Such a decline in our purchases from other nations could not but have a serious effect upon their employment. It seems safe to say that the aggression of Germany and Japan, which lies at the base of this

163

war, are not unrelated to the severe depression that prevailed in this country during the 1930's. We must, if we expect peace and order in the other nations of the world, see to it that our economy does not continue to fall periodically into a morass such as we floundered in during the past decade.

We turn now to a consideration of the basic problem as to why we have unemployment. The primary question is, Why do we have difficulty in selling the product that we produce? The answer, as I see it, is that our habits of saving quite necessarily lead to an accumulation of savings that outrun investment opportunities and are therefore left uninvested.

Uninvested savings—idle money funds—mean that workers must be idle too, unless such a large volume of new money is being created, as during the present war, that the accumulation of idle funds is more than offset.

This idea, which was marked economic heresy for a hundred years, has recently become almost a commonplace. Economists are increasingly stressing the need of having savings invested promptly, and businessmen are making this same point. Only recently Mr. Sloan, chairman of General Motors, for example, insisted in a public address that savings be invested very promptly. This is the kernel to the general analysis developed by John Maynard Keynes of England, which has had such a profound effect upon the thinking of economists throughout the world and upon the fiscal policies of many nations.

Thus we come to the point that it is essential that we shall have continuous investments in order that the savings which we make will be used promptly. Continuous investments means that we must have what is commonly spoken of as "expanding economy." If our economy did expand sufficiently to absorb all of our savings, all would be well so far as employment is concerned. This is a very big IF. One might as well say: IF the people of the nation always kept well, there would be no problem in respect to the furnishing of medical services. For both in terms of the historical record and of theoretical analysis the conclusion is inescapable, it seems to me, that investments cannot be made continuously. Certainly the record is clear. Throughout our history we have come to the end of profitable investment opportunities every few years. At least, men have stopped making investments; workers have been dismissed; and the well-known downward spiral of deflation has set in.

The analysis that I have been able to make leads me to the conclusion that such a result—the failure to find investment opportunities—is the inevitable result of our savings habits under our present economic institutions. That is, it seems to me that the depressions with which we have been cursed have not been caused by the failure of competition, by monopolization, by protective tariffs, nor by mistakes of businessmen, but have come because of the savings-investment process as we practice it. Depressions will come, if my analysis is sound, regardless of how perfect we may make our competitive process and regardless of how capable the economic advisers are whom the businessmen employ to tell them what to do.

VI

My analysis is briefly as follows. It may be wrong, but here it is. Investments yield consumption goods. They must do this if the investment is to justify itself socially or is to pay in a momentary sense. The extra goods which are thus produced by new investments, if all other things are equal, can be purchased only by the persons or firms who made the investments. But they do not want to buy consumption goods. They want only investment goods—more investment goods. But since they will not buy the extra consumption goods, markets are congested, and there is no profit to be made from making further investments. Thus unemployment and depression are inevitable.

To illustrate the point that it is only the investors, all other things being equal, who can buy the extra goods which are produced as a result of the investments, consider a case in

165

which a small economy has full employment which is maintained by the purchase of all that is produced. Now suppose that Mr. Z saves $2,000 and lends it to a businessman, who employs labor to fashion a piece of equipment that increases output by $100 worth of goods. Suppose further that the bank lends the businessman $100 on the security of the extra goods. This supposition eases the problem of selling the goods. The $100 is paid to Z as interest on his loan. With all other things being as before, who can buy the extra $100 worth of goods? The answer is clear; only Z can buy them. If he will buy them, the market will be cleared and employment can be maintained. But if Z wishes to save the $100, the goods cannot be sold and production will be curtailed and employes dismissed.

I do not see any escape from this conclusion. If savers would buy—if they would consume—the extra product which their savings make possible, as pioneer farmers consumed apples when the trees they had planted began to bear, employment could be maintained. But when they attempt, as is the general rule with us, to save the income from their savings, a market impasse becomes inevitable.

The day of doom to the usual period of prosperity is usually postponed by the use of several devices. The extra goods which only the savers have the money to buy are sold on credit to the spenders. Following the liquidation that takes place during a depression, we may continue to increase the amount of consumer credit outstanding for seven or eight years. This is of the greatest possible help in maintaining a period of prosperity. From 1923 to 1929, inclusive, for example, we increased the consumer debt by five and a half billion dollars. That is, for eighty-four months we sold, on an average, more than 60 million dollars' worth of goods each month to persons who could not pay for them and who had not paid for them when the decline began late in 1929.

Another device is to sell abroad more goods than we buy from abroad. This relieves the pressure on our markets. During the years to which I have just referred our net export of goods amounted to the same total as the increase in outstanding consumer credit. Here we had another 60 million dollars' worth of goods which we took out of our markets every month, on an average, during these years. Adding these two items together, we have 120 million dollars' worth of goods which we got rid of each month on an average. Here in small compass is the explanation of why the period of the 1920's was so prosperous.

But the extensions of credit, both at home and abroad, must come to an end. When this happens, prosperity gives way to depression. That honeymoon is over. For when we save persistently—when we save the income from savings instead of consuming it—consumer goods will congest the market except as devices such as those that we have noted give us a breathing spell of a few years.

Another way of looking at this is to note that saving the income from savings means to save at compound interest. But since this is a finite world, any compounding must be sharply limited. Consider the matter of plants and animals, including human beings. No one of these forms of life could double very many times. There just is not enough room. A doubling of our population only four times would give us more people than there are now in the entire world. Or, to have begun in the year 1 with only one couple and to have doubled the population every twenty-five years would have brought the population of the world by 1925 to 189,000,000 persons for every square foot of the land area, including mountain peaks and swamps. That would be too many people. This is a finite world.

Similarly, there are sharp limits upon the compounding of interest. One cent placed at 6 per cent interest in the year 1, to compound annually, would have amounted by the end of 1943 to a sum equal to the value of six billion billion balls of pure gold the size of the earth. This shows that compound interest is absolutely impossible over very many years. No one

167

family could long compound its savings. The very nature of the finite world prevents it. Yet we build our economy upon compound interest and expect the observance of the Ten Commandments to save us from our folly.

What happens, of course, is that in the realm of plants and animals death takes place along with new life. It is only thus that new life is possible. Similarly, attempts to save at compound interest mean that losses must take place. Economic death must offset gains at interest. But the prevalence of losses dampens the ardor of investors, savings are held uninvested, and unemployment results.

VII

This general condition is vividly illustrated by the amazing prosperity which we are now experiencing during the war. In spite of having put ten million persons in the armed services and having devoted the labor of millions of others to the production of war goods, we have, it seems, produced more consumers goods than ever before. *Fortune* magazine estimates that in 1943 we consumed 16 per cent more goods and services than in 1939, after adjusting for price changes. This is amazing.

Why have we been able to do this? Because there has been a ready market for everything that we could produce. The government has stood ready to buy from fifty to ninety billion dollars worth of war goods and service each year, and the receipt of money from the government has given buying power to the public with which to buy all of the consumer goods that could be produced. Recently there has been much pointing with pride to what "free enterprise" has done. But it is not free enterprise that has done this amazing job. It is free-managed enterprise producing for a war market that has done it. Private business has not secreted the buying power to make this output possible. And cannot do so under our present savings habits.

The difficulty which we have in selling the goods which

we produce also explains why we could not take payment for the debts owing to us through the government at the close of the first World War. Foreign nations stood ready to pay us more than 14 billion dollars. Did we ease the way for them to pay? Indeed not. We promptly raised our tariff and ten years later raised it again. We pounded the table and insisted that we be paid, but we saw to it that we were not paid in the only coin that the foreign nations could pay in—goods.

This difficulty which always confronts us explains our present worry about the goods that will be left over at the close of the war. We fear these goods like a plague. For if they are allowed in our markets there will be danger of widespread unemployment.

Similarly, we could not take indemnities from Germany or Japan. We do not want the goods that they might furnish us. We have difficulty enough selling the goods to ourselves which we produce.

Russia, however, will not have any trouble at all using all of the goods that Germany may furnish her. According to the reports, the Russians will demand not only huge payments in goods but also large armies of workers. The point is, of course, that the Russian economy is one of government ownership and hence is not troubled with the problem of distributing the product. There is no more difficulty on that score than there was on a large self-sufficient pioneer farm. They can consume all that they can produce, or all they can get from outside. If they find themselves eating too much, they can simply shorten hours.

But, to repeat, with us the savings-investment process, together with the necessity that business firms must meet money outgo, means that we must periodically sink into a depression. This means that the peace of the world will continue to be endangered; for unemployment here tends to be contagious in every capitalist country, and unemployment carries the seeds of revolt and war.

We need to do all that we can to lessen the ravages of our

depressions. Many of the devices that we have instituted during the past twelve years will be found helpful in the depression periods that lie ahead. Particularly the prompt creation of government deficits and the expenditure of the newly created money in providing employment will be helpful. But these, after all, will be only palliatives. We shall still have depressions.

We need to alter our savings-investment process. The proper adjustment here will not only cure the disease of chronic and depression unemployment; it will also remove the struggle for export markets, including fields of foreign investment, and thus eliminate the problem of competing tariffs. The alteration of each of these aspects of our economy in the manner indicated will lessen the tension that directly and indirectly incites nations to war. It is to this problem that you young citizens must address yourselves in the years that lie ahead. The proper solution of it will mean freedom from the curse of unemployment at home and increased opportunity for peace throughout the world.

COMPETITION AND MONOPOLY IN THE POSTWAR WORLD

CLAIR WILCOX

Professor of Economics, Swarthmore College

AMERICAN INDUSTRY HAS DOUBLED ITS PRODUCTION OF GOODS and services in the past four years. Its present output for war is as great as our entire national product in any year before the war. And, on top of this, it is producing more civilian goods and services than it did before Pearl Harbor, twice as many as it did in the trough of depression—in 1932.

One can only speculate upon what we could have done with this tremendous output if we could have devoted it to purposes other than waging war. We are now producing enough to provide every family in the United States with an income of $5,000 a year. We have demonstrated beyond doubt that we have it within our power to abolish poverty; to provide all of our people with health and decency in housing, clothing, nutrition, and medical care; to afford real equality of educational opportunity; and to insure security against unemployment, sickness, and old age. And this miracle of production has been worked, in lesser degree, by other nations that are now at war.

Will the postwar world permit its productive capacities to serve the purposes of peace as fully as they have served the purposes of war, or will it insist upon a return to prewar levels of output? Will it organize its industry for expansion or for restriction? Will it seek to stimulate production or to retard it? This is the issue with which we are here concerned. And it is an issue that needs to be raised, insistently and repeatedly. For the provision of plenty is a postwar ob-

171

jective that ranks close in importance to the preservation of peace.

There are two methods by which this goal may be approached. One requires the socialization of industry and the direction of production by an all-powerful state. The other involves reliance upon private enterprise and the operation of free markets. It is true that many promotional, regulatory, and supervisory functions have been assumed by nonsocialist governments; but this fact does not destroy the fundamental contrast between these two extremes. The Soviet Union is clearly committed to the first of these courses; there may be other peoples who will adopt her system in the years that follow the war. Most of the nations of the world, however, are avowedly committed to private enterprise. What are the prospects for production in each of these economies?

A socialized economy, in Russia or elsewhere, may conceivably provide the masses of its people, in rapidly increasing quantities, with the goods and services that they would freely choose. But there is no assurance that it will do so. Its controls will certainly be cumbersome. Its industry, lacking the spur of competition, may well be inefficient. Its governors are likely to postpone technological innovation and resist economic change. Under dictatorship, instead of responding to the free choices of the people, the socialized economy will inevitably serve the purposes of the dictator, whatever they may be. Under democracy, if there should ever be a democratic socialist state, it would lend itself to the exploitation of the consumer in the interest of producing groups.

In their capacity as consumers, all men have a common interest in enlarging the total income of the economy by expanding production. But in his capacity as a producer, each man belongs to a group that has a special interest in enlarging its share of that income by restricting production. The common interest is usually unorganized, inarticulate, and impotent. The special interests are always well organized, vocal, and powerful. The result is that the machinery of demo-

172

cratic government has all too often been employed to reduce the output of industry in an effort to preserve the occupations and to maintain or increase the incomes of various producing groups. In the democratic government of a socialized economy, there is reason to believe that such restraints would be intensified, since all decisions affecting producers' occupations, output, and incomes would be made by agencies of the central state. When production and price are fixed politically, there is little likelihood that they will be fixed in the public interest. The hope of the consumer lies in the diffusion, not in the concentration, of power.

By contrast, the promise of an economy of private enterprise and free markets is great. The case for private enterprise has often been stated. It is a system under which businessmen assemble capital and labor and direct them toward production of those goods and services that have been freely chosen by consumers. It makes for economic progress because it keeps the door open to new products and new processes, to new materials and new machines, to new blood and new ideas. It eliminates waste, enhances efficiency, and cuts costs. It raises quality, reduces prices, and brings about an ever-widening distribution of the products of industry. It thus combines the greatest possible economy in the utilization of resources with the greatest possible satisfaction of human wants.

The whole case for private enterprise rests, however, upon one fundamental assumption: that effective competition shall prevail. There must be several sellers in every market; there can be no barrier to the entry of new concerns. Each seller must act independently; there can be no understandings, explicit or implicit, concerning production or price. This should be obvious, since it is clear that the monopolist is under no compulsion to improve quality, to cut costs or prices, or to distribute increasing quantities of goods. In so far, therefore, as the postwar markets of the private-enterprise economies are effectively competitive, it is possible that something approaching the present levels of output will be maintained. But in so far as they are monopolized, it is probable that production will be curtailed. It is necessary, therefore, in appraising postwar prospects, to examine the forces that are likely to make for effective competition and those that will make for noncompetitive restraints.

Before the war there were few industrialized countries, outside of the United States, in which the production and sale of manufactured goods was effectively competitive. In Japan, where industrialism had been imposed upon a feudal society, the control of industry was in the hands of a few great families. In Germany, France, Belgium, and Italy, and elsewhere on the continent of Europe, the control of major industries was concentrated in giant combines and the production and distribution of manufactured goods was regimented by powerful cartels. Through these agencies European business fixed prices and terms of sale; divided productive activities, markets, and customers; limited production; assigned quotas in output and sales; and enforced its regulations by the imposition of penalties. The control of European manufactures has been further concentrated in the hands of German industrialists during the war, through a continuing process of amalgamation, through the Aryanization of Jewish firms, and through the Germanization of business in conquered territories, all of it accomplished with scrupulous regard for legal forms, much of it camouflaged by the protective coloration of Swiss incorporation, and all of it directed toward the service of the Nazi state.

In Great Britain, where the policy of freedom of trade had long impeded the progress of cartelization by compelling British businessmen to meet the competition of foreigners, the abandonment of that policy, following the first World War, provoked the most rapid transition to a predominantly cartelized economy that the world has ever seen. British trade associations, on the eve of the second World War, were busily engaged in fixing prices, buying up and retiring productive capacity, limiting output, assigning quotas, pooling earnings, and using these pools to reward those who restricted output and to penalize those who increased it. Britain's complete conversion to the German cartel system was dramatically demonstrated on the two days which followed Hitler's invasion of Czechoslovakia in March of 1939, when representatives of the Federation of British Industries and the Reichsgruppe Industrie, meeting in Düsseldorf, agreed to substitute "constructive co-operation" for "unhealthy competition" in the export trade of the two nations by having individual industries conclude restrictive agreements, as some fifty had done or were ready to do, and to take the lead in bringing other nations into the scheme—if necessary, by enlisting the aid of their respective governments.

The consequences of such cartelization are clear. By establishing prices at levels that are calculated to cover the costs of their least efficient members, cartels remove the incentive to introduce improvements and eliminate wastes. By assigning quotas on the basis of present capacity and past output, they freeze production to existing locations and obstruct adjustments that might cut costs. In both of these ways they operate to maintain capacity in idleness, to curtail production, and to prevent consumption from reaching levels which it might otherwise attain. Instead of facilitating economic progress, they make for stagnation and decay.

In the United States there are many fields that, in the absence of public intervention, are predominantly competitive. Among them are agriculture, fisheries, lumber, bituminous coal, textiles, leather, apparel, foods, furniture, and many other consumers' goods, and most of the wholesale, retail, and service trades, comprising altogether as much as half of the nation's business. At the other extreme there are a few industries that have been almost completely monopolized. These include aluminum, magnesium, nickel, shoe machinery, glass-container machinery, and electric-lamp manufactures, and telephone, telegraph, sleeping car, electric light and pow-

175

er, and other utility services. But neither of these situations is typical of such largescale manufactures as iron and steel, copper, lead, and zinc, chemical and petroleum products, cement, glass, automobiles, farm machinery, bottles, tin cans, electrical equipment, photographic materials, fountain pens, typewriters, refrigerators, sewing machines, meat, sugar, soap, thread, movies, tobacco, cigarettes, and chewing gum. In each of these industries, a few concerns control the bulk of the output and dominate the field. The four largest producers account for three-fourths or more of the output in the case of nearly one-half of the products that are manufactured in the United States.

In such fields competition has characteristically been restrained by common stockholdings; by interlocking relationships; by explicit or implicit agreements to share markets and fix prices; by the practice of obtaining patents and refusing to grant licenses, or granting licenses on restrictive terms; by the extension of monopoly power to unpatented products sold by patent owners, to unpatented products made on patented machines, and to subsequent stages of production and sale; by the maintenance of elaborate systems governing the quotation of delivered prices; and by the simple practice of following the price leader.

In those fields where firms are more numerous and smaller and where the degree of concentration is relatively low, competition has been restrained by trade-association activities which closely parallel the practice of the British associations and the European cartels. Curtailment of output has been encouraged by the circulation of statistics on capacity, production, inventories, and orders. The establishment of common prices has been facilitated by the standardization of cost-accounting forms, methods, and costs. Direct price cutting has been discouraged by systems which require the filing of price quotations; and indirect price cutting has been prevented by the standardization of commodities, guarantees, discounts, and terms of sale. In some cases, associations have allocated markets, assigned quotas governing output, and fixed minimum prices; and these arrangements have been enforced by penalties and by boycotts which were designed to discipline price cutters and to whip nonmembers into line.

In those fields, finally, where producers are so numerous and so small that they cannot establish and enforce such arrangements through their own efforts, competition has been restrained by procuring the enactment of laws which curtail output and fix prices, at the expense of the consumer, in the interest of members of the producing group. So we have had the late and unlamented N.R.A., the agricultural adjustment program, the prorationing of petroleum, the establishment of minimum prices for milk and trucking services and bituminous coal, the legal maintenance of resale prices and the prohibition of sales below cost in the retail trades, the many interferences with the movement of goods between the states, the employment of sanitary laws and building codes to circumscribe local markets, and the use of discriminatory taxes to exclude outsiders from a pre-empted field.

In all of these cases producers have sought, not to achieve full employment of the nation's resources, but to protect established occupations and investments. They have attempted to serve this purpose, not by taking a small margin of profit on a large volume of output, but by taking a large margin on a small volume. Instead of cutting prices to distribute their potential product, they have maintained them and wasted resources on costly methods of promoting sales. In all of these ways they have used their power over production and price, not to promote industrial activity, but to retard it.

These restraints within domestic markets have their counterparts in the restrictions that producers have imposed on international trade. In fact, the two are intimately related. For, unless, high tariffs or shipping costs prevent it, monopolistic arrangements in domestic markets may be destroyed by competition from abroad. And, unless domestic markets are effectively controlled, international monopoly may be destroyed by competition at home.

The tightest form of control over world markets is that accomplished through the international combine. In this case, the holding-company device is commonly employed to bring under common ownership and management a number of enterprises that have been incorporated to operate in different countries. Thus, the International Telephone and Telegraph Company holds stock in cable, radio, and telephone companies throughout the world; and its subsidiary, the International Standard Electric Corporation, controls companies engaged in the manufacture of communications equipment in many different states. In a similar way the N. V. Philips organization has crossed national borders to control concerns which manufacture and distribute electrical equipment and supplies. More recently, the I. G. Farbenindustrie has absorbed the manufacture of dyestuffs in France; and the Herman Goreing Works has come to dominate the iron, steel, copper, armament, construction, and shipping industries throughout much of Europe.

A looser form of organization than the combine, the international cartel may be equally effective in eliminating competition in export trade. Such an association may fix prices directly or influence them indirectly through agreements which reduce capacity and allocate output, markets, and sales. These restrictions are frequently enforced by systems of deposits and fines and by boycotts which cut nonmembers off from markets and supplies. Hundreds of these agencies were formed during the period between the two world wars. American concerns, organized into export-trade associations under the provisions of the Webb-Pomerene Act, participated in cartels which controlled the sale of copper, steel, sulphur, potash, rubber thread, and many other goods.

International cartels are frequently based upon agreements with respect to patent rights. In such an arrangement American firms are licensed under patents which foreigners have obtained in this country and foreign concerns are licensed under patents which Americans have obtained abroad. The terms of these licenses may divide territories, limit output, and fix prices. The foreign partner will agree not to sell in the American market; the American partner will agree not to sell in the foreigner's market; the two of them will agree upon a common policy to govern sales in the other markets of the world. And all of these arrangements will be enforced under the patent laws of countries involved. In this way markets for chemicals have been divided among I. G. Farben, Imperial Chemicals, and Du Pont; those for magnesium between I. G. Farben and the Aluminum Company of America; those for synthetic rubber and gasoline between I. G. Farben and Standard Oil of New Jersey; those for tungsten carbide between Krupp and General Electric; and those for electric lamps between General Electric and the European lamp cartel. Similiar arrangements have obtained in the markets for aluminum, zinc, plastics, fertilizers, rayon, pharmaceutical products, photographic materials, and optical glass.

Like the domestic cartel, the international cartel operates to bar new enterprise, to obstruct technological improvement, to impair productive efficiency, to check consumption, and thus to hold down planes of living. Like the tariff, it operates to restrict imports and exports. But unlike the tariff, it is set up by businessmen, without public representation or responsibility, through secretly negotiated traties, for private ends. It thus delivers the determination of foreign policy into the hands of private supergovernments. If at the end of this war the victorious Allies were to choose to reduce their tariffs in the interest of world peace, their policy might well be defeated through the erection of private tariffs by international cartels.

In international as in domestic markets for raw materials, where producers are numerous, small, and scattered, pressure is brought to bear on governments to organize and enforce restraints. So there have been many schemes for international commodity controls. Limitations have been imposed upon acreage sown, livestock kept, and minerals developed, and, at a later stage, upon crops gathered, livestock slaughtered, and mines worked. In cases where production could not readily be curtailed, portions of a crop have been destroyed. Exports have been restricted through taxation, prohibition, the imposition of quotas, and the requirement of licenses. Subsidies have been paid and loans made to assist producers in withholding their supplies. Governments themselves have bought, stored, and held commodities in an effort to maintain their prices. Such shemes have been applied to coffee, rubber, sugar, tea, tin, and wheat. Nominally they have been devised for the purpose of stabilizing prices. But the levels at which this stabilization has been attempted have invariably been higher than those that could be justified by conditions of demand and supply. Production has been frozen to uneconomic locations. High-cost operations have been subsidized. The consumer has footed the bill. Indeed, no other line of policy could have been expected in a program whose producer motivation was so plain.

On the eve of the second World War the markets of the private-enterprise economies were thus subjected to a series of restraints that condemned them to a level of production far lower than that which they might otherwise have attained. The tremendous increase in output that has accompanied the war must be attributed, not to private enterprise, but to the fact that expansion has been ordered, directed, and financed by the warring states. What will happen when this artificial stimulus has been removed? Will private enterprise, in vigorous competition, maintain production at levels never previously realized in times of peace? Or will the productive energies of the peoples of the world again be shackled by noncompetitive restraints?

As far as Germany and Japan and the occupied countries are concerned, no one knows. The unconditional surrender of our enemies will raise new questions, provide us with no answers. Are the giant German combines to be left in possession of Europe's industry? Are the present owners of this industry to be allowed to retain their control through Swiss holding companies? If not, how are the combines to be dissolved? How are the holding companies to be attacked? Are expropriated properties to be left in the hands of their present owners? If not, can the rightful owners be found, their claims verified? If not, will ownership be socialized? If not, how will it be transferred to private hands? Will European cartel agreements be allowed to stand? If not, will they be smashed? Will the liberated countries acquiesce in such a policy? If not, can it be carried out? Is Japanese industry to be left in the hands of four great families? If not, what is our plan for the reorganization of the industrial life of Japan?

In Great Britain the outlook for competition is far from bright. Britain will emerge from the war in a seriously weakened condition, with her overseas investment sold, her great merchant marine lost, her industry run down, and her export markets sacrificed to new competitors—without her normal means of earning the very food she eats. In the circumstances, it is not surprising that the leaders of British business appear to face the future without hope, that they seek to achieve salvation, not through energetic competition at a high level of output, but through financial security at a low level. As a consequence, the future policy of Britain is now the subject of a vigorous debate.

The attitude of British industry is clear. It has been expressed repeatedly and forcefully by every representative organization of businessmen in the British Isles. And it adds up to this: Free competition, both in the domestic market and in foreign markets, is gone forever. Every British industry is to be organized into a powerful trade association on the model of the German cartels. These associations will plan production, control materials and sales, divide markets, and fix prices. Membership may be made compulsory, and the associations may be given power to make and enforce their own rules. A national council of industry will be empowered to handle relations between the trade groups and the government. Each of the national associations will belong, in turn, to an international association or cartel. And these cartels, consisting only of private business interests, will control the exports and imports of every industry and regulate every commodity that moves in international trade, determining productive capacity, output, inventories, and export tonnages; dividing world markets; and fixing a world export price. At the top of the pyramid there will be a world-wide agency, representing business alone, which will buy up export surpluses and lend-lease them to backward countries so that the fixed prices will not be endangered by increasing supplies. The only function of governments will be to enforce these private arrangements as they have done in the past in the cases of commodity agreements and patent cartels. All of this is covered, of course, with a gloss of protective verbiage. Poverty is to be abolished, standards of living are to be raised, and general employment is to be assured by curtailing the output and raising the prices of every industry on earth. Against these proposals a few men—notably Mr. Herbert Morrison and the editors of the London *Economist*—have spoken with clarity and force. The outcome of the debate remains in doubt.

In the United States there are many developments that point toward a revival of competition in the postwar years. We have enlarged our productive plant: we are now equipped to produce twelve times as much aluminum and seventy-five times as much magnesium as we produced before the war. We have kept small business alive; our policies in subcontracting and in price control have favored the survival of the smaller firm. We have increased the number of enterprises engaged in certain fields: aluminum ingot, once a complete monopoly, is now produced by three concerns. We have made rapid strides in technology: the lighter metals, alloy steels, plywood, plastics, and unbreakable glass must now compete with one another in many markets; there is little prospect that they will be subjected to unified control.

But forces opposed to competition have also been generated by the war. Our military orders have been highly concentrated: seventy per cent of the business has gone to one hundred large concerns. Our corporations have accumulated substantial reserves; they will be able to sit out a postwar depression instead of cutting prices to maintain their sales. The war's end will leave great stocks of many goods in public and private hands; the size of our productive plant will be without precedent; business believes that these factors threaten to flood our markets with supplies that will depress prices and destroy profits, a view that may well give rise to demands for some sort of a postwar N.R.A.

In this situation everything depends upon the policies of our government. Shall we hold surplus war goods off the market as a means of maintaining highly profitable prices, or shall we release them at a rate that will stimulate healthy competition in price? Shall we padlock, dismantle, or export our publicly owned war plants, or sell them to monopolies for a song; or shall we sell or lease them to new enterprises or, failing this, operate them as yardsticks in order to provide fresh competition for established firms? Shall we raise tariffs to protect new industries or lower them to promote trade? Shall we strengthen our antitrust program, or shall we abandon it?

If antitrust is to be adequately implemented, there are many things which we should do. We should repeal the many statutes that operate to exclude competitors from markets, to handicap the efficient seller, and to protect the inefficient: the state laws that permit resale price maintenance and prohibit sales below cost, the federal Miller-Tydings Act and certain provisions of the Robinson-Patman Act, the discriminatory taxation of chain stores, and the numerous barriers to trade between the states. We should repeal the Webb-Pomerene Act, which facilitates American participation in European cartels. We should abandon the prorationing of petroleum and the establishment of minimum prices for agricultural products and for bituminous coal. We should permit motor carriers and water carriers to compete for traffic on equal terms with carriers by rail. We should reform our patent system, strengthening the Patent Office; establishing higher standards of patentability; shortening the term of the patent grant; requiring public registration of sales, assignments, and the terms of patent licenses; and supervising foreign patent licenses and patent pools. We should strengthen the Anti-Trust Division and the Federal Trade Commission and proceed vigorously to enforce the laws forbidding restraint of trade.

Nor are these the only weapons that we have at our command. We could compel the licensing of patents and prohibit the inclusion of restrictive provisions in patent licenses. We could require federal incorporation and federal supervision of corporate financial practices. We could apply to nonutility holding-company structures the same program of simplification and regulation that we have applied in the utility field. We could discourage monopoly and encourage competition by altering our taxation policies.

There is nothing inevitable about monopoly. It usually finds its origin, not in the superior economy of size, but in artificial arrangements and special privileges: in intercorporate connections, open agreements, secret understandings, restrictive contracts, discriminatory prices, and unfair methods of competition; in permits, licenses, patents, and tariffs; in the exclusive ownership of scarce resources; and in laws that limit output, fix prices, and handicap competitors in the interest of politically powerful producing groups. These are matters that are subject to control. If our policy requires it, we can have an effectively competitive economy in the United States.

What are the prospects for such a policy? In America, the issues of postwar economic organization have not been publicly discussed. It is true that the spokesmen of business have been asserting, repeatedly and emphatically, that we must return to an economy of private enterprise. But they have failed to propose specific measures to restore the competitive conditions which their positions would logically require. Organized agriculture, moreover, is clearly committed to guaranteed prices and legalized restraint of trade. And organized labor has displayed little interest in the problems of competition and monopoly. Our people have been vocal on the questions of war and peace, of depression and unemployment; but on issues involving the volume of postwar output they have had little to say.

With respect to world markets, it appears that we shall not agree to put our trade in the strait jacket of international cartelization. On the contrary, it is likely that we shall use our bargaining power to persuade other nations to co-operate with us in breaking up and regulating international combines, in preventing the use of national patent systems to divide world markets, and in prohibiting the restrictive practices of international cartels. And, failing this, it is probable that we shall forbid our manufacturers to participate in cartels that are set up abroad.

In the case of raw materials, however, there are straws in the wind that are less encouraging. Our government agreed, at a meeting of the foreign ministers of the Latin-American republics in January, 1942, to buy up supplies, over long periods, at prices that will be "remunerative to producers," so that "producers are protected against competition from products originating in areas wherein real wages are unduly low." It is a party to the International Wheat Agreement, which provides in detail for the limitation of production and stocks and for the establishment and enforcement of export quotas and a minimum price. And it joined with others at the United Nations Conference on Food and Agriculture in June, 1943, in recommending the creation of an international organization to set up similar schemes for other commodities.

If it is true, as the conference asserted, that the world is suffering from hunger, malnutrition, and starvation, one wonders why it is that we are planning to restrict our food supply.

The direction of our policy is still in doubt. The ways that lie before us are three. The first leads to an economy of private enterprise, the second to an economy of private collectivism, the third to an economy of public regimentation. But the second and the third of these roads must ultimately converge. For concentrated public power will challenge concentrated private power and, though the struggle may be long and bitter, the state will finally prevail. The line that we will take will depend upon the leadership of our national administration; the character of our Congress; and the attitudes of business, agriculture, and labor. At the moment, it is impossible to predict with certainty what the outcome will be.

The issue, however, is plain. Are the world's resources to be employed to meet the crying needs of its peoples, or are they to be imprisoned to enhance the profits of producers? Are science and invention to be allowed to bear fruit in rising planes of living, or are they to be condemned to sterility? Is private enterprise to have a new lease on life; or, is it, at last, to be laid to rest, unwept, unhonored, and unsung?

INTERNATIONAL ORGANIZATION AFTER THE WAR

Manley O. Hudson

Judge of the World Court

THE GENERATION OF WHICH WE ARE A PART FACES A STAGgering challenge. For a second time in a bare quarter of a century most of the peoples of the world are engaged in a destructive and horrible world war. Must the human race continue to be defeated by more world wars? The spirit of man cries out for a better way of life.

New hope has come to us with the Moscow Declaration, of October 30, 1943, calling for the establishment of "a general international organization . . . for the maintenance of international peace and security." If we are to win this war, it seems quite clear that we must take that step.

Two questions must be in our minds, however. Is there a will among the peoples of the world to find escape from recurrent world wars? And can a way of escape be found? It is the second of these questions with which I propose to deal, not in the role of a prophet but in the role of a student who has devoted most of his lifetime to a study of international organization.

Fortunately, we have many proposals before us today. Some of them are serious, some are "crack-pot." We need to maintain toward them a critical attitude. At the same time, if we would make any contribution to American thinking on this matter, we must have a constructive approach also.

In my attempt to maintain a critical attitude, I find it necessary to remind myself continually of a few simple truths. I am in constant danger of losing myself in a mass of facts or in a labyrinth of theories, and I have set down for my own guidance three propositions which I repeat to myself each morning as I get up and each night as I go to bed.

First, I have to remind myself that the world did not begin yesterday. It is a disturbing thought, at times, for everything would seem so easy if we could write on a clean slate. Yet you and I know that we live in a stream of history. Some of my friends talk as if, once the battles are won, we shall have but to wave a wand and our problem will be solved. Yet wands have been waved before in human history, by men as intelligent, as devoted, and as farseeing as any of us. If now we would go beyond their efforts, we must know what they have attempted, what they have achieved, and wherein were the reasons for their failures.

Second, I must not let myself forget that the world will not stand still tomorrow. Not a pleasant thought, at times; for our task would be so much simpler if we could assure ourselves that, once we have put the world into order, it would stay put. Yet all of us know, though I am in danger of forgetting it, that change is inevitable. Twenty-five years ago we fought, and we were told we won, a war to end war. Italy and Japan were our allies in that high enterprise, and both of them have been arrayed against us in our present struggle. Any plans we make now must take account of such shifts in national policy; no line-up of nations will be everlasting.

Third, I find it necessary to say to myself over and over again that the road to international affairs is not a one-way street. It is a perplexing thought, and I often want to escape it. If we could think of the maintenance of peace as dependent on our national policy alone, the job would seem so compassable. Many of my friends seem disposed to approach it in that way. Yet you and I must know that a policy adopted by one great nation can so easily be emulated by other great nations. Large armaments, colonies, bases all over the world, autarchy—whatever is the order of the day for our own people, or for a few of the peoples of the world, can also become

188

the order of the day for other dynamic peoples. No one people can have a monopoly of aspiration to power and riches.

With this approach, I must, of course, appraise our experience with international organization during the past hundred years. In the middle of the nineteenth century it was an American postmaster general who proposed the creation of a league of nations to deal with postal communications—that league has existed now since 1874, and it has given us a world-wide system of postal exchanges. In 1865 an international telegraph union was formed, and it still exists as the International Telecommunications Union. Various other unions were formed in the nineteenth century, and they were followed up in the constructive work of the Hague Peace Conferences in 1899 and 1907. The Permanent Court of Arbitration, established in 1899, survived a world war and continues to exist today—I have the honor to be a member of that Court on appointment of President Roosevelt.

Then we come to the great era of international organization which followed the War of 1914-18. Through the League of Nations almost all of the states of the world—all except a few diminutive ones—were enlisted in various co-operative efforts. Sixty-three states became members of the League. Through the International Labor Organization these states have pushed forward a great work of social reconstruction. Through the Permanent Court of International Justice a great advance has been made in the administration of law in the relations of states.

Now what can we say of this history? I must say that it constitutes a great chapter of human experience, and as such we cannot ignore it. These efforts, these advances, must be the cornerstone of our building for the future.

What lessons emerge from the experience? I suggest, first of all, that it has demonstrated a need for universality in international organization. No piecemeal approach will suffice. No lines can be drawn which would shut some states out. A league of democratic states would soon find itself confronted by a rival and hostile league of nondemocratic states.

Secondly, I suggest that no generation can solve all of the problems which will arise in international affairs, and that each generation will insist—as ours insists—on meeting its own problems in its own way. What can be handed down from generation to generation is agencies, methods, and procedures by which solutions may be sought. We of this country are the beneficiaries of institutions handed down to us by preceding generations—yet the Congress and the Supreme Court of the United States serve very different functions from those envisaged for them one hundred and fifty years ago.

A third lesson which I would draw from the experience is that the problem of the use of force in relations between states must be faced honestly and squarely. The Covenant of the League took a revolutionary step when it declared that a war anywhere is a matter of concern to peoples everywhere. If we have the will to peace, we must seek to realize that principle—and, of course, we must admit that it may have to be applied to ourselves. We must realize that in modern wars all the peoples engaged deem themselves to be acting in self-defense, and hence any people's use of force must be subjected to a common judgment. This involves some control of armaments, and it necessitates our development of methods for the pacific settlement of all international disputes.

If we are to act upon these lessons from experience, the general international organization promised in the Moscow Declaration presents us with a great opportunity. Without the support of the United States no attempt, I believe, will be made in this direction. With that support the job may proceed without our worrying about many of the problems which we have debated during the past twenty-five years.

I present such a course to you, not as a matter of cosmopolitan thinking, not as altruism, not as a poet's dream. In our time international organization has become a stark necessity if we are to seek either security or prosperity for ourselves.

AMERICAN ATTITUDES AND LEADERSHIP

HAROLD H. BURTON

United States Senator from Ohio

THE SPIRIT IN WHICH WE APPROACH OUR NATIONAL AND international issues is all-important. I emphasize five civic virtues which, when practiced, have accounted for much of America's rise to unique influence in the world. I recommend their practice today. Two are typified by George Washington, two by Abraham Lincoln, and the fifth by both of them and by millions of Americans "known only unto God."

Shortly before his inauguration as the first president of the United States, Washington wrote to his friend General Knox: "Integrity and firmness are all I can promise." Those virtues thus became the foundation stones of the character of the Republic. They are essential to a sound personal, national, and international character. President Washington was the living embodiment of them.

Integrity requires men to be honest both with themselves and with the world. It requires them to speak the truth and to keep their word. It is only thus that men and nations can become dependable, and international stability can be built only upon dependability. The nearer men and nations come to having deserved faith in one another, the nearer will they come to peace on earth.

Firmness is a product of integrity. Only he who tells the truth can afford to be firm. With truth as a foundation firmness is natural. These civic virtues fixed the form and cast the features of our early body politic.

Three generations later Lincoln became so much a part of America that today we cannot describe our national

191

character without emphasis on some characteristic of his. He added to American public life qualities as important to it as those which the New Testament added to the Old. He demonstrated the outstanding value of fairness and kindness. He developed a human and understanding heart in our body politic.

The fifth and most fundamental virtue of the five is that of reverence for God and man. Too often forgotten today, reverence for God, coupled with a deep appreciation of his equal fatherhood of all men, greatly influenced the spirit of America in the days of the making of the Mayflower Compact, the Declaration of Independence, the Constitution of the United States, and the Gettysburg Address. Such reverence not only has filled the hearts and minds of our leaders but has united the efforts of countless men and women who by their faith and works have made America a beacon of hope for mankind everywhere. Such men and women are the sinew and the soul of our body politic.

In her international relations it is important that America be genuinely herself and that she approach her postwar international problems with integrity, firmness, fairness, kindness, and reverence. If she does less she will not be true to the purpose for which America was founded. We are a nation built on faith in God and man. Our Declaration of Independence was not a document claiming territory. It was not a document claiming rights in the name of a sovereign. It was a declaration of faith that governments derive their just powers from the consent of the governed and are instituted among men to secure to each one of them certain inalienable rights with which they have been endowed by their Creator, including especially their respective rights to life, liberty, and the pursuit of happiness. As Lincoln so clearly interpreted this statement, this declaration was not limited to men in any one place or of any one time or race. In 1858 he said that it applied to "the whole race of men," and "to the economy of the universe." He said it represented a "noble understanding of the justice of the Creator to his creatures." And, referring to the beliefs of our forefathers, he added:

In their enlightened belief, nothing stamped with the divine image and likeness was sent into the world to be trodden on and degraded and imbruted by its fellows. They grasped not only the whole race of man then living, but they reached forward and seized upon the farthest posterity. They erected a beacon to guide their children, and their children's children, and the countless myriads who should inhabit the earth in other ages. Wise statesmen as they were, they knew the tendency of prosperity to breed tyrants, and so they established these great self-evident truths, that when in the distant future some man, some faction, some interest, should set up the doctrine that none but rich men, none but white men, or none but Anglo-Saxon white men were entitled to life, liberty, and the pursuit of happiness, their posterity might look up again to the Declaration of Independence and take courage to renew the battle which their forefathers began, so that truth and justice and mercy and all the humane and Christian virtues might not be extinguished from the land; so that no man would hereafter dare to limit and circumscribe the great principles on which the temple of liberty was being built.

This is the attitude of deep faith in the cause of man with which America should approach her new problems in the world-wide field of expanding human relations as she did in 1776 in the field of her newly declared national independence.

We are a nation founded in the interest of the individual man and dedicated to his freedom and advancement as fast as circumstances will permit. This purpose we must apply to the changing needs of our time. Our horizons expand, but our guiding star remains the same. Our numbers grow, but the sacredness of each human soul is preserved. "America is not so much a place as it is a people." It is primarily a human institution established for the benefit of human beings. As beneficiaries of a great past and trustees of a greater future, we of America must constantly rededicate ourselves to human

193

service worthy of our increasing responsibilities and opportunities.

We are looking now into the dawn of the most critical year of our generation. It is for us to meet its tests with faith and vigor fully equal to those of our forefathers and thoroughly consistent with the purposes and principles of which our government is the product.

In the field of action, decisive military victories are our first essential need. Whatever we say or do about postwar plans must be so said and done as to help win the victories that will make peace possible. It should be so said and done as to add new strength and unity to the efforts of the United Nations to win the war as quickly and completely as possible in both hemispheres. At the same time failure to make tangible progress with plans for the peace while fighting the war would be as serious a failure in our civic duties as if our generals failed to plan their next military campaigns while fighting the battles of today. Timing and preparation are as important to peace as they are to war.

Peace involves thirty-four United Nations, about ten Associated Nations, three or more enemy nations, and in some degree all other nations. This totals over sixty nations and over two billion people. On such a scale the horizons of antiquity or even of a generation ago disappear. We speak, we see, and we act around the globe. We think of and deal with more men at a time than ever before. Our opportunities and responsibilities have expanded together. We catch a new sense of the need for a world-wide devotion to the practice of the Golden Rule under conditions that have made all the world a neighborhood.

In our postwar international relations we shall be dealing with subject matters comparable to those with which we have been accustomed to deal but on a larger scale and with greater means for quick and widespread action than ever before. We must adapt our technique of government to the new needs and speeds of our time. We must meet the novel demands for constructive action with the same courage and faith that filled the hearts and minds of our forefathers when they met the novel demand of the men and women of the thirteen original states for some new procedure that would reflect the will of the governed in national as well as local affairs. With the principles of the Declaration of Independence in their hearts and their hard-won freedom at stake, they met in the Constitutional Convention at Philadelphia in 1787. No one took to that convention the plan that came from it. Yet from that convention came the Constitution of the United States, which has been a source of infinite strength to us and a model of infinite value to free men everywhere. While today there are some similarities to that situation as the United Nations face the problem of international stability with their hard-won freedom again at stake, yet there also are great differences between the two situations. I mention the earlier experience, not so as to copy the solution then reached, but rather to draw from that experience the lesson that if men will face new problems in the light of great principles and with an invincible determination to find solutions worthy of the opportunities, they may be able to create new and workable plans of human relations that will preserve the peace for a long time and thus justify somewhat the infinite price paid for that peace.

Several steps already have been taken. I mention three and quote three statements from them. The first is the Atlantic Charter of August 14, 1941; the second is the Declaration by the United Nations of January 1, 1942; and the third is Senate Resolution 192, adopted by the Senate of the United States of America, November 5, 1943, incorporating in it a part of the Moscow Agreement of October 30, 1943.

While the Atlantic Charter is but a joint declaration of the personal points of view of the President of the United States of America and the Prime Minister of the United Kingdom and has not been incorporated in a treaty between those nations, yet it has received such formal and informal world-wide recognition that any step that departs from it will call for a justification of such departure. I quote its sixth paragraph, which states: *"After the final destruction of the Nazi tyranny, they* [the President and the Prime Minister] *hope to see established a peace which will afford to all nations the means of dwelling in safety within their own boundaries, and which will afford assurance that all the men in all the lands may live out their lives in freedom from fear and want."*

On January 1, 1942, twenty-six nations joined in the Declaration by the United Nations. Since then eight more have adhered to it. I quote the Preamble to this declaration because of the subscription to the Atlantic Charter there expressed by all the signatories. It says: *"The Governments signatory hereto, having subscribed to a common program of purposes and principles embodied in the Joint Declaration of the President of the United States of America and the Prime Minister of the United Kingdom of Great Britain and Northern Ireland dated August 14, 1941, known as the Atlantic Charter, . . .* declare" that each government pledges itself to employ its full resources to fight those with whom it is at war and not to make a separate peace.

On November 5, 1943, by a vote of 85 to 5, the Senate of the United States adopted Senate Resolution 192, which incorporated as its fourth paragraph, word for word, the fourth paragraph of the Moscow Declaration of October 30, 1943, entered into by representatives of the governments of the United States of America, the United Kingdom, the Soviet Union, and China. This paragraph states: *"That the Senate recognizes the necessity of there being established at the earliest practicable date a general international organization, based on the principle of the sovereign equality of all peace-loving states, and open to membership by all such states, large and small, for the maintenance of international peace and security."*

It is notable that these provisions emphasize the need for unity of action among all of the United Nations, large and small, the need for action that will create a living organization capable of meeting the changing needs of the future, and that the last statement emphasizes the need for early action along these lines.

As indicating further active consideration of these issues by the twenty-one American republics, including the United States of America, I quote also the following:

First, Resolution XXV on Postwar Problems, adopted at the meeting of the ministers of foreign affairs of the twenty-one American republics at Rio de Janeiro and released February 2, 1943, resolves:

To request the Governing Board of the Pan American Union to convoke an Inter-American Technical Economic Conference charged with the study of present and post-war economic problems, and

To entrust the Inter-American Juridical Committee with the formulation of specific recommendations relative to the international organization in the juridical and political fields, and in the field of international security.

Next, Resolution XXXV, adopted at the same meeting, resolves:

To take note of the contents of the "Atlantic Charter" and to express to the President of the United States of America its satisfaction with the inclusion in that document of principles which constitute a part of the juridical heritage of America in accordance with the Convention on Rights and Duties of States approved at the Seventh International Conference of American States, held at Montevideo in 1933.

Finally, as demonstrating the thinking even in 1939 on the relation of these republics to the world, we find the following "Joint Declaration" issued by the ministers of foreign affairs of these republics at that time:

The inter-American system is not founded on any spirit of isolation, nor is it in any sense antagonistic to any other section of the world or to any other international organization. The American Republics feel that they have a set of problems peculiar to themselves, and that these can best be solved by cooperative action among the several states. At the same time *they recognize the interdependence of the world as a whole, and the inevitable necessity of every state and region maintaining contact with and being influenced by developments in every other state or region. The American Republics have therefore adopted a series of rules and principles to govern their relations with non-continental states and regions. These rules and principles are free from any selfish purpose of isolation, but are inspired by a deep sense of universal cooperation.*

Dedicated as America is to the cause of personal liberty as opposed to perpetual slavery, we eliminate from our program any plan for a lasting peace comparable to a Pax Romana based upon conquering and enslaving the world by the aggression of any one or more of the United Nations. Similarly, the United States sees the inevitable failure which has attended efforts to keep forever in balance the shifting power of one group of nations as against that of another group of nations. The system of balanced powers probably has prolonged many an armistice. However, when changing weights of the respective powers have upset the balance, new and greater wars have followed. For these reasons, the above declarations and the logic of our time suggest, as the next step toward a just, a lasting, and a living peace, the formation of an international organization open, at least, to all of the United Nations, large and small, and probably providing a means for the later acceptance of all nations of the world. This organization shall have as its primary objective that of establishing and maintaining the peace and security of the world.

The United Nations, when victory comes, will have demonstrated, by that victory, that as long as they remain united there is substantial assurance of military peace and security. On the other hand, if this "championship team" of World

War II disintegrates to any degree, there is created immediately a corresponding degree of uncertainty as to the future. Regardless of the reason which may cause any nation, large or small, to withdraw from the United Nations, such withdrawal will produce at once a need on the part of every other nation to offset that uncertainty. This will lead naturally to alliances and counteralliances until the pattern of the next war is written in them.

More important, therefore, to the peace of the world than any other national or international policy of America or of any other nation is this essential need to insure continued unity among the United Nations. It exists now in time of war. As long as it exists among all the United Nations, the assurance of military peace and security as against outside aggression is reasonably sure. The primary obligation of every peace-loving nation is to see to it, therefore, that this unity continues in time of peace. To this end, it is important that there be no period of uncertainty following the relief of the United Nations from the pressure of common danger from the enemy. This makes it correspondingly important that at least preliminary understandings leading toward peacetime unity shall receive widespread advance consideration and approval before the coming of the peace. The chances of reaching such understandings probably are better in time of war than they will be in time of peace. Today each of the United Nations is under substantial pressure to find a way to maintain its unity with each of the others so as to insure its own safety and so as to help to win the war. This immediate pressure will end with the war.

It is appropriate to recall, at this point, that, apart from any new organization of the United Nations and apart from any new understandings for the establishment and maintenance of peace, the United States already is a party to hundreds of treaties and to scores of international working arrangements helping to meet the current needs of our time. These official working arrangements cover many questions

199

relating to legal matters; labor problems; agricultural, industrial, and financial relations; communications; health and social conditions; standards and statistics; art, science, and education; to say nothing of the military boards reaching into production and distribution of materials; and to say nothing of an organization of such general scope as the Pan American Union dealing with many international interests of the twenty-one American republics. The day of complete isolation for the United States, or for any civilized nation, has in actual fact long since disappeared. There can be no question but that the United States wishes to take full advantage of the scientific, commercial, industrial, agricultural, and cultural developments of modern civilization. As an isolated nation, America cannot do this any more than a hermit living alone in a cave can keep up with the opportunities and standards of living in the modern world. The freedom, national independence, and sovereign equality of a civilized state does not mean that it shall live apart from the world. Its freedom includes freedom to exercise its judgment to enter into treaties, contracts, and agreements with others to the mutual advantage of both parties, just as the individual citizen of today improves his standards of living and his opportunities by specializing in his labor and by taking active part in a state of society in which he depends in large part upon others for many of his needs, while they in turn depend partly upon him for their needs.

Modern standards of living depend upon international relations. These depend upon many international agreements and undertakings. These benefits, however, are of little value if the world frequently is forced to fight desperately to defend itself from slavery. The primary duty, therefore, that we owe to those who are paying the infinite price of victory today is to see to it that some means is found to keep the victorious United Nations united in peace as well as in war. Such an organization of the United Nations must then draw into itself all of the other nations and peoples, large and small, so that, except for the outlaw, there will be none left outside to wage aggressive war against them. As for any outlaw nation, it must be restrained and resisted as effectively by the society of nations as the individual outlaw today is restrained and resisted by the organized governments of today. He is not exterminated, but he is so effectively restrained and resisted by community force that his own lawlessness becomes a minor nuisance rather than a major danger.

Even the tragedy of two world wars in the same generation may be worth the price paid to win them if the people of the world shall gain from them a clear understanding that the world's first obligation to itself is to maintain unity and stability among substantially all the nations of the world. The form of the unifying organization is not as important as the fact of the unity. This brings us directly to the question as to what the next step toward such unity should be and who should take it.

The Moscow agreement and the Senate resolution previously mentioned point the way. The first step was spelled out in Senate Resolution 114, introduced nearly a year by two Republican and two Democratic senators. The substance of it was included in Senate Resolution 192 as adopted in November, 1943; but the November resolution omitted any plan of procedure, whereas the earlier proposal stated what should be done and who should do it. It proposed that the United States take the initiative in calling meetings of representatives of the United Nations for the purpose of forming an organization of the United Nations with specific and limited authority as there stated.

This is the step needed to be taken now. In recent months there have been meetings between leaders of the four major United Nations. These have been helpful. We also have seen a recent gathering of representatives of the United and Associated Nations resulting in the formation of the United Nations Relief and Rehabilitation Administration. This has been helpful.

It is important, however, that long before the armistice arrives, the nations of the world, large and small, determine upon an elemental course of procedure which shall be followed as the fighting stops so that there always shall be an orderly continuance of united action among the United Nations. It may be necessary to defer agreement on the final form of the organization in many particulars, and it may be well to leave for the future the determination of many regional problems. We should, however, soon agree upon an orderly method of procedure through which the nations of the world, large and small, shall recognize that there is before them a road to a just, a lasting, and a living peace under which they may look for procedure marked with attitudes of integrity, firmness, fairness, kindness, and reverence even though agreement on the precise form of organization may be postponed until circumstances shall permit of more clear representation of the wishes of many of the peoples directly affected. In the meantime, separate international agreements can be reached on such urgent and separable issues as those of international civil aviation and international exchange which may be essential to the economic stability of the world regardless of its political organization.

Next come the questions as to who shall initiate this step and where shall these meetings be held. It may be well for the initiation of the meetings to come jointly from the nations who are bearing jointly the primary burdens of the war—namely, Britain, China, Russia, and the United States. But even then leadership must come from somewhere among these four in suggesting the initiation of these meetings. I believe that this responsibility falls upon the United States of America. America's long-standing friendly relations with most of the other nations of the world and her freedom from suspicion of imperialistic motives makes her leadership especially natural. The place of the meetings is not vital but might well be within the United States of America. Ours is the only one of the lands of the larger United Nations which is free from the scourge of war. Our facilities, therefore, are now more readily available for activities of this kind than are those of our allies. Furthermore, of the thirty-four nations now constituting the United Nations, fifteen of them are in North, Central, and South America, including the Dominion of Canada. The remaining seven of the twenty-one American republics might well take such an occasion as this to voice their formal adherence to the Declaration by the United Nations. This would result in twenty-two of the forty-one United Nations being located in the Western Hemisphere.

Within the United States we have the equally important problem of taking governmental action leading up to the step which I have suggested and leading up to the full and cordial support of the plan by the people of the United States. To this end it is vitally important that at once there be increased unity of action and understanding between the executive and legislative branches of our own government on questions of postwar stability both domestic and international.

The internal stability of the United States, quite as much as its hemispheric and international stability, depends upon the establishment and maintenance of the peace of the world. If America is to carry a $300,000,000,000 national debt without default, as she must, and if America is to develop the necessary earning power to carry that debt and to maintain reasonable prosperity at home, it is essential that there be peace and stability in the world. It is only when we have such peace and stability that we and our allies can dare to reduce substantially our postwar military and naval expenditures.

For the American people to see the vital importance to their own industrial and agricultural recovery and to their own security against another great war, it is essential that our national administration take the people genuinely into its confidence and demonstrate deep faith both in the people at large and in their elected representatives.

203

Not long ago the United States of America was a small nation seeking the same freedoms for herself that she now supports for all peace-loving nations. If the United States is to live up to her full responsibility for her own peace and security and live up to her ultimate ideals for the individual man, she should take the course indicated. She should soon call to her aid leading representatives of her own people. With their loyal co-operation she should then initiate meetings among representatives of the United Nations to be held here in the interests of further consolidating their united efforts in winning the war completely in both hemispheres and in furthering the establishment at the earliest practicable date of a general international organization based upon the principle of the sovereign equality of all peace-loving states and open to membership by all such states large and small for the maintenance of international peace and security.

This is the obligation of the people of America to their forefathers and to their children and their children's children. It is the natural obligation of America as a leader in the cause of freedom and progress of the individual man.

When General MacArthur was welcomed to Australia, he replied: "I have come as a soldier in a great crusade of personal liberty as opposed to perpetual slavery. . . . There can be no compromise. We shall win or we shall die, and to this end I pledge you the full resources of all the mighty power of my country and all the blood of my countrymen."

That is the pledge that is being redeemed on the front line. It is for all of us to match that standard. Let each of us make this pledge: We are soldiers in a great crusade of personal liberty as opposed to perpetual slavery. We shall see to it that there shall be established and maintained a just, a lasting, and a living peace, so that, when our soldiers and sailors return from the front, they and their children and their children's children can enjoy here the America of which they think, of which they dream, and for which they fight.

BIOGRAPHICAL NOTES

HASTINGS EELLS

Now professor of history at Ohio Wesleyan University, Dr. Eells is a Presbyterian minister as well. He holds degrees from Clark, Princeton, and Yale universities and did graduate work at the University of Brussells and the University of Ghent. After a three-year pastorate in Pennsylvania he joined the faculty of Ohio Wesleyan. Many of his summers have been spent as visiting professor at Duke University and at Pennsylvania State College. He is the author of a number of books, including *Martin Bucer* (1931) and *Europe Since 1500* (1933).

ROBERT S. LYND

COLUMBIA UNIVERSITY's Robert S. Lynd, professor of sociology, has had a richly varied experience as writer, soldier, businessman, scholar. A native of Indiana, he was educated at Princeton University, Union Theological Seminary, and Columbia University. After four years as editor of the *Publishers Weekly* he served with the field artillery in 1918. On return to civilian life he became manager of advertising and publicity for the book department of Charles Scribner's Sons. From 1927 to 1931 he was secretary of the Social Science Research Council. With his gifted wife, he wrote the significant and widely read study *Middletown—A Study in Contemporary American Culture* (1929), which was followed by *Middletown in Transition* (1937) and *Knowledge for What?* (1939).

JOSEPH L. HROMÁDKA

DR. HROMÁDKA was formerly a professor of the John Huss faculty at Charles University in Prague, Czechoslovakia. He is now guest professor in the Stuart chair of apologetics and Christian ethics at Princeton Theological Seminary.

THOMAS A. BISSON

BEST known as the author of *Japan in Asia* (1938) and *American Policy in the Far East: 1931-1941* (1941), Dr. Bisson is a member of the research staff of the Institute of Pacific Relations and an associate editor of *Pacific Affairs*. After study at Rutgers University and Teachers College, Columbia, he was from 1924 to 1928 a missionary teacher in China. He joined the research staff of the Foreign Policy Association in 1929. Taking a year's leave of absence, he returned to China in 1937 on a fellowship from the Rockefeller Foundation for study of the Far Eastern situation. He was principal economist of the Board of Economic Warfare, 1942-43, before joining the international secretariat of the Institute of Pacific Relations.

BIOGRAPHICAL NOTES

FRANCIS B. SAYRE

UNITED STATES High Commissioner to the Philippines from 1938 to 1942, Dr. Sayre escaped from Corregidor by submarine in February, 1942. He is at present diplomatic adviser of the United Nations Relief and Rehabilitation Association. His educational and diplomatic background includes study and teaching at Williams College and Harvard University Law School; diplomatic experience in Siam, 1923-29; and service as assistant secretary of state in charge of American trade agreement, 1933-39. He is the author of numerous international trade agreements and some dozen books, the latest of which is *The American Trade Agreements Program.*

Y. C. YANG

DR. YANG is the president of Soochow University, China. He served in the Chinese diplomatic service from 1915 to 1922. During that time he was secretary of the Chinese minister at Washington and attaché of the Chinese legation at London. He worked with the Chinese delegation at the League of Nations and with the Chinese delegation at the Washington Disarmament Conference. From 1922 to 1927 he served with the Chinese Ministry of Foreign Affairs. In 1927 he was elected president of Soochow University. Temporarily unable to function as president because of the Japanese occupation, Dr. Yang has recently been Tallman Professor of Chinese Civilization at Bowdoin College, Maine, and is now director of the speakers' bureau of the Chinese News Service. He is the author of *China's Religious Heritage* (1943).

VERA MICHELES DEAN

MRS. DEAN is research director of the Foreign Policy Association, New York. She is a graduate of Radcliffe College, with a master's degree in international law from Yale University and a Ph.D. from Radcliffe. Since 1928 she has been with the research staff of the Foreign Policy Association, specializing in Russian and Italian affairs and problems of European diplomacy. She edits all the Association's research publications and has written many of them herself. She is co-author of *New Governments in Europe* (1934) and author of *Europe in Retreat* (1939).

HENRY A. ATKINSON

DR. ATKINSON is general secretary of the Church Peace Union and the World Alliance for International Friendship Through the Churches. Before coming to the present post he served a number of Congregational churches as pastor, was professor of sociology at Atlanta Theological Seminary, and for eight years was secretary of the Social Service Commission of the Congregational Churches in the United States. He is co-author of *The Causes of War* (1932) and author of *Prelude to Peace* (1937).

JOHN L. CHILDS

PROFESSOR of the philosophy of education at Teachers College, Columbia University, since 1937, Dr. Childs is considered an expert on Russia. He graduated from the University of Wisconsin and received his M.A. and Ph.D. degrees from Columbia. From 1916 to 1927 he was foreign secretary of the international committee of the Y. M. C. A., Peiping, China. He is the author of a number of books on education and is co-author of *America, Russia, and the Communist Party in the Postwar World* (1943).

H. GORDON HAYES

SINCE 1920 Dr. Hayes has been professor of economics at Ohio State University. He had previously taught at Hiram College, the University of Michigan, the University of Minnesota, and Yale University. In 1928 he was visiting professor at the University of Puerto Rico. He was chief of the division of economic research of the Bureau of Foreign and Domestic Commerce in the year 1934-35. His best-known piece of writing is the two-volume work *Our Economic System* (1928).

CLAIR WILCOX

DR. WILCOX is professor of economics at Swarthmore College. He was formerly director of the Industrial Materials Division of the Office of Price Administration and consulting economist of the Social Security Board. He is a contributing editor of the *St. Louis Post-Dispatch*.

MANLEY O. HUDSON

A JUDGE of the Permanent Court of International Justice since 1936, the Hon. Manley O. Hudson has had a career amazingly full of personal achievements and public usefulness. Previously a professor of law at the University of Missouri and at Harvard University Law School, he has since 1923 been Bemis professor of international law at Harvard. He served as special assistant to the Department of State, 1918-19; as attaché of the American Commission to Negotiate Peace, Paris, 1918-19; and as a member of the League of Nations secretariat, 1919-21 and the summers of 1922-33. Since 1924 he has been the editor of the *American Journal of International Law*. Besides the books he has edited, seven works on international law have come from his pen. His *Handbook on the World Court* reached its fifth edition in 1938, and a revised edition of his substantial *Treatise on the Permanent Court of International Justice* was issued by Macmillan in 1943.

HAROLD HITZ BURTON

SENATOR BURTON of Ohio is a native of Massachusetts. He was educated at Bowdoin College and Harvard University Law School. In the first World War he saw active duty in France and Belgium as a captain in the United States Army. After long legal practice in Utah, Idaho, and Ohio, he served as mayor of Cleveland from 1935 to 1940. He has been United States senator from Ohio since 1941.